PRAISE FOR
OUTRAGEOUS EMPOWERMENT

"I learned at an early age to 'model the masters' when it came to business success. Ron Lovett, in *Outrageous Empowerment*, tells it like it is. In his storytelling fashion, Ron doesn't deliver us theory, but rather, take aways we can implement immediately to accelerate our success."

Jack Daly, Amazon Best Seller, Sales Guru and Serial Entrepreneur

"Ron overcame bigger industry challenges than Southwest Airlines or Starbucks—an incredible feat."

Len Preeper, President and CEO of Thinkwell Research

"Finally, there's a 'how-to' on getting your staff aligned on purpose, values and key metrics so all your people are beating the same drum. This book was a game-changer for my organization."

Shaun Majumder, Actor/Comedian and Social Entrepreneur

OUTRAGEOUS
EMPOWERMENT

OUTRAGEOUS
EMPOWERMENT

THE INCREDIBLE STORY OF

GIVING EMPLOYEES THEIR BRAINS BACK

RON LOVETT

This book is dedicated to the staff of fifteen hundred plus that helped me realize how much potential they had that I didn't know about. I'm grateful for all the authors, speakers, and corporations that inspired me to take bits of their knowledge along the way.

It's also dedicated to all the CEOs, leaders, and managers in companies with a large frontline staff. You are all blessed with an ocean of untapped human resources available to you, right on your frontline—the people that are interacting with your customers face-to-face and gathering crucial information to innovate every day. Don't let this go to waste. Believe in them and allow them to flourish—don't be me and wait ten years to realize their potential.

CONTENTS

FOREWORD

I suppose you're thinking it's terribly unorthodox for an author's wife to write a foreword for a business book, but in fairness, being unorthodox captures the book's essence, so perhaps, it's quite fitting.

When I met Ron Lovett, he had a tremendous back-story involving several entrepreneurial ventures (most of them legal); and he had a way of communicating with people of all backgrounds that made them feel important.

At the ripe age of twenty-two, Ron did what he does best: he dove head first into completely unknown waters. Surprisingly enough, this wasn't the scariest part of his journey. After over a decade of operating quite similarly to his competitors in the security industry, he realized that if he didn't start innovating, he was simply going to lose.

The security industry was challenging, to say the least. There were terrible margins, accompanied by a sales process that was almost always driven by the lowest bidder. Security guards shuffled from one company to the next depending on where the work was, so company loyalty was practically non-existent. And given the nature of turn-around time when you did land a contract, the hiring process basically consisted of anyone who had two arms and legs and was willing to do it. Site managers had become accustomed to being minimum-wage babysitters. Minor fires were reported on a daily basis, but problem solving for the company from the frontlines was something foreign to the industry and typically left to the CEO. Sound familiar yet?

Needless to say, a culture built on family values and collaboration wasn't something that seemed attainable.

After a couple of financially devastating years, Ron decided that in order to find personal enjoyment in his business once again, he needed to turn the industry on its head. No process, company hierarchy, or personnel type was to stay as it was. Everything would be done differently. If it wasn't broken, then they would break it anyway and put it back together in a way that was completely contrary to the industry.

People began to think that Ron was a visionary—an entrepreneurial genius that had something nobody else did. But I saw the simplicity of it all. I was, of course the one who had the pleasure of eavesdropping while he cooked dinner, or listening to his "why in the world has no one done this yet?" rants he spewed every morning from the shower.

New competitors were finally on his radar. He wanted to compete with Starbucks in regards to customer experience. Southwest Airlines was his newest target as it pertained to frontline workers and their company culture. And then, of course, there was Uber, who had revamped a transportation industry without any parameters in terms of how they did the work.

One day I asked, "But honey, these companies are in completely different industries—how are they relative?" Sometimes I'd think he'd gone off the rails.

"That's the whole point," he said. "I hate how the security industry operates, as do my people—all of them—from the frontline security guards to the management staff. That's why we need to start looking at things through a different lens. We need to start fresh for the entire industry."

Now, this was the most daunting challenge Ron had ever been faced with. If he was wrong about how to reinvent this stale industry, it would mean closing his doors. We were looking at starting a family right around this time, so tackling something of this magnitude was extremely scary for me as well. But no amount of cautionary tales would stop this train—he was already on it, and recruiting everyone around him to jump on board.

Ron took it process by process, dissecting how everyone's work was completed, and how those employees felt about the daily tasks at hand. He began to see traction, and then regression. The cycle repeated itself, and I continued to watch the internal struggle of what felt right to him, but was not necessarily translating into dollars.

Until one day, Ron gave a security guard from Toronto the task of purchasing the next company vehicle. That security guard researched the best deals, models and contracts in terms of what made sense to the market there. The security guard struck a chord with Ron. Ron felt like he had given a minimum wage worker their brain back, and the results were powerful.

Alignment. It was that simple. If he could tap into the unused potential of his over fifteen hundred employees across the country, he could create a security business that was for the first time, truly aligned. It would have to flow through their people, their processes, each department and their recruitment strategy. But it was possible.

My conversations with Ron over dinner slowly morphed into much more positive discussions. The fear began to subside, and he found momentum by converting his staff into stakeholders in the company. People were now actually loyal to the brand because the brand finally stood for something, and those core values that were originally taped on an 11" x 13" poster on the boardroom wall were now being painted in the main foyer of their head office, and truly internalized by the fifteen hundred employees who were actually living them every day in their work.

Though our family dinner time was often interrupted by staff from all across the country calling Ron's cell phone to discuss new opportunities and share their stories, I knew then that something great was occurring, and my husband's ability to execute was unlike anything I had ever seen. If something was working, he did more of it, immediately. If something was not working, he changed it, immediately. No smoke and mirrors, or genius at play—just the ability to execute faster with a fearlessness that no one saw coming.

Natalie Owens
Atlantic Canada-born Sales Professional

INTRODUCTION

I haven't always been good at first impressions. After two decades in the private security business, I have survived my fair share of wild encounters—some more smoothly than others. There was the time merchant banker and reality TV star, Mike Wekerle, asked me to help him set up booby traps in his friend's house, with the intention of soaking his pal with water when he opened the front door. It was only after our plan worked that I learned we were in the home of Tie Domi, the legendary NHL bruiser. I also learned Tie didn't like surprises any more than he liked having water dumped on him in his own home. He chased us around the living room while throwing jabs and hooks at our legs and ribs for half an hour. There was also the time I showed up to lead a security team for then-U.S. vice president Al Gore, wearing a swollen nose and black eye after an encounter with a group of rowdy bouncers went sideways the night before. And how could I forget one of my first high-profile gigs, leading Ringo Starr to the wrong hotel room, on the wrong floor, only minutes after meeting him and days after raving to myself about how great I must be to land such a famous client. "Jesus Christ, you couldn't guard a dead body, could you?" Ringo joked. I had never been more embarrassed in my life.

I've always had a knack for finding a way to turn garbage into gold. From my lifelong struggles with acute dyslexia and attention-deficit/hyperactivity disorder (ADHD), to a childhood raised by a single mom and hanging around bad crowds from low-income neighborhoods in Halifax, Nova Scotia; to my experiences transition-ing from juvenile delinquent to nightclub bouncer, to the president and "chief support officer" of Canada's leading security company, I learned that where you start does not determine where you finish. Being different, as it turns out, offers each of us a greater capacity to do better than the norm. Only you can decide what you will or will not accomplish in your life, your career, and your industry, and for those willing to leverage their differences and embrace the uncertain-ties of change, there are no limits to your journey. It won't be easy, of course, but I truly believe anything is possible, so long as you turn the volume down on those who tell you otherwise. You will need to ignore, or even part ways with a great many people, but that's okay. It only makes it easier to find the doers and the visionaries, those explorers and trendsetters who provoke meaning and forge paths where none existed.

My own beginnings have sparked a lifetime of searching for the best tricks, advice, and opportunities in my effort to take the path less traveled and get to the top on my own terms. Part of that path is found by reading books and listening to the journey of others. I wouldn't be where I am today without all of the information I was able to gain from such sources. I know I don't have all the answers, but I do have a story to tell you about why you don't need to have them all in the first place.

The following pages serve as a snapshot of what I learned from all the ups and downs, the mistakes and successes, and the wild times I experienced while building, leading, and personally negotiating the sale of Source Security to one of the largest security services companies in the world at the age of thirty-seven. This is my story on how to hire the right people, align them around one common purpose, and set them free to do things they love outside their day-to-day functions.

This added tremendous value to our business, and I truly believe it can add value to yours too—whether you are a business owner, entrepreneur, employee, or student.

This book is a product of my unconventional ascent from a certain dead-end to a life I couldn't be more grateful for. One whose challenges and limits seem smaller, its meaning deeper, and its future brighter. I hope you will find inspiration and encouragement from the lessons that follow to improve your insight and skills, and to shape a more positive frame of mind. I also hope you will find the process much easier than taking a few punches from Tie Domi or embarrassing yourself in front of a Beatle. After all, there's no sense in making the same mistakes twice!

STARTING AT THE SOURCE

CHAPTER 1

MY FATHER AND PABLO

"I knew Pab," my father told me. "And George Jung was a punk. We used to do bigger loads than him."

I was eighteen at the time, engaged in an online chat with the father I'd never met, and already he sounded like a huge story topper. He and my mother had separated when I was about three months old, shortly before my mother returned to her native Canada with my sister and me.

I guess I shouldn't have been surprised, really. Looking back, my father claiming to be an obscure drug-dealing legend, second to no one in Pablo Escobar's long list of associates—not even Jung, who by all accounts was the largest cocaine importer to North America throughout the 1970s and 1980s—wasn't all that outrageous. But I was young and found the thought of him and his past alluring in the dangerously cool kind of way that rebellious teenagers tend to love. That might explain why my mother had never been eager for me to meet him.

As a kid who had spent his entire life on the working-class side of Halifax, Nova Scotia, I wanted more. I wanted to travel and explore the world. I wanted to build something incredible, do something so spectacular it would inspire everyone around me. I wanted to have the things none of us ever could. Reflecting on it now, I mostly just wanted to be the kind of person I'd always wished I had in my life when I was growing up. That was the ultimate pull. It's what made heading three thousand miles away to meet a man who at least sounded like he had been incredibly successful at something, anything—even if it was smuggling drugs—seem like a really good plan. Besides, I had already met plenty of real gangster types around my neighborhood, so the idea of a cocaine dealer wasn't particularly disturbing. For two years, I tucked away the cash I made from cutting hair, delivering newspapers, and selling pot in the neighborhood. Then, I bought a plane ticket to Orlando.

Just before I left Halifax, my mother reminded me that my father had never seen a picture of me after the age of three. A year earlier, my mother had given me a silver bracelet that had once belonged to him, and I had held on to it ever since. To make sure we found each other, my mother instructed me to wear it—an ID of sorts for my father to recognize at the airport.

Several hours later, I was wandering around a terminal in the Orlando International Airport looking for a man I'd never seen before. Then, out of nowhere, a large voice rang out, "Hey, son!" A man stood in the stream of travelers, his arms held out wide, dark aviator sunglasses shielding his eyes, and a grin stretching halfway across his leathery face.

I froze, a little confused, assuming that I had been mistaken for someone else.

"Well, come on. Give me a hug, son!" He charged forward and wrapped his burly arms around me, squeezing hard until I dropped my luggage and gulped. Then, he hoisted my duffel bag from the floor, slung it over my shoulder, and slapped me on the back as if we'd only been apart for a week rather than a lifetime. "Whaddaya say we get outta here, huh? I bet you're hungry."

Over the next few hours I listened to stories of how things might have been, and how his absence and lack of support was the fault of someone else. I knew then what I'd tried to ignore all along was true: no matter how it's packaged, bullshit always smells the same. I knew a hustler when I met one, because, as it turns out, back in those days, I was one, too.

But let's start at the beginning.

SCRAPPERS AND SELLERS

Resting along Canada's Atlantic coastline, Halifax is a small city and the capital of Nova Scotia. Founded in 1867, Nova Scotia is one of Canada's oldest official provinces, but Halifax's colonial history extends even further back, to the arrival of British and French Protestants a century earlier. Today, the city's deep Scottish and Irish roots give Halifax its strong sense of cultural identity. Central Canada's decades-long grasp on finance and manufacturing built an economy wholly different from Atlantic Canada's dependence on trade and natural resources. And with those economic differences came differing work societies, with central Canada's geared around management— a mentality and skill set necessary for sustaining success rather than building it. Along much of the eastern coast, however, long lines of Scottish and Irish settlers relied on an aggressively self-reliant and enterprising spirit to survive. Today, there's still a certain grit that permeates the air, left over from those early years. It's an attitude that couples a fierce commitment to autonomy with a communal effort to achieve it. On the opposite side of the spectrum, a stubborn defiance toward change fills the streets, sometimes teetering on hopelessness. And yet, despite the naysaying resistance of some, the majority of Haligonians possess a jovial, compassionate, and enterprising spirit.

It was in this region that I was raised, steeped in the dualities born of a people's entrepreneurial DNA and dejected sense of themselves. After my parents separated, we left Florida to live with my aunt in Halifax, and later with my grandmother, nearby. My mother's side of the family was mostly hardworking, blue-collar type that is so prevalent in Halifax. They were tough, straight shooters who were generous yet streetwise, proud and humble all at the same time—and from them I learned firsthand that nothing worth having in life would come easily.

For several years after we relocated, my mother's work demanded that she spend most nights on the road, leaving my sister and me under the charge of our grandmother. One day, while digging through boxes, I came across a stash of my father's old photo albums. Cessna airplanes, yachts, Porsches, and luxury homes filled the pages, triggering my curiosity at the time: what happened to this stuff? That box became a window into a world outside my own, one that I would turn to often as I began to wonder about my future, and about my father.

When I was seven years old, my mother married again, and for a time, we lived happily as a normal family. My stepfather gave my sister and me his last name, and he offered us the structure of an average household. But what began as discipline quickly devolved into verbal abuse, prompting frequent and heated arguments between my mother and stepfather. As I grew older, the tension between my stepfather and I grew thicker. We fought constantly, and though I was terrified of him, I always found ways to get back at him. Farting into his bottle of mouthwash was a favorite and perfected tactic of mine.

To escape the turmoil at home, I took to hanging out in the streets with other kids like me: young and restless, desperate to belong somewhere. It wasn't long before I was getting into trouble, and shortly after my thirteenth birthday I was detained for my part in vandalizing a car. A few years later I was arrested for theft, and a short time after that, my mother and stepfather discovered I was growing pot in the house to sell around the city. They weren't as mad about the pot as they were about the expensive power bills they had been paying for months. It was also one of my earliest business lessons: considering every step of the business and what the surrounding factors will be. In this case, I had totally missed that round-the-clock electricity meant higher overhead costs—even if they were on my parents' dime. I guess you could say I was ambitious in all the wrong ways.

Along with the legal troubles, I was largely detached from my schooling, tallying what must still be a record-setting number of absences and poor grades during my junior high and high school years.

On the outside, it appeared as though I was heading for prison, or worse. I didn't really know it at the time, but below the surface, I was actually laying the foundation for many of my future entre-preneurial pursuits. Throughout my early teens, I held three paper routes. When I was fifteen, I set up a barbershop in our attic and started cutting people's hair for five bucks.

A year later, I read a finance book by Garth Turner called *How to Build Wealth and Retire in Comfort* and learned that with a registered retirement savings plan (RRSP), someone could begin saving money at forty and be a millionaire by the time they were sixty-five. Of course, my first thought was: "Hey, if I start saving at sixteen, then I'll be rich by the time I'm forty!" The next day I went into my local Bank of Nova Scotia branch with fifty dollars in hand and opened an RRSP account, to the surprise of the bank manager and staff.

"Why do you want to do this?" one of them asked.

"Well, it says here in this book that if I start saving today, I'll be rich in thirty-five years," I said. "So, I want to get started today."

I was always trying to find a way to pave my own path. Back then, I didn't know exactly what I was going to do, but I did know a few things. I knew that at some point I wanted to have invest-ments in real estate, and I knew that I wanted to be an entrepreneur with my own operating company or companies. I didn't know what those companies would be yet, but having those goals clear at an early age served as a guide away from my current circumstances and as a purpose beyond my own self-destruction.

Poor grades, fighting, and excessive absences all contributed to a few suspensions during high school, but I somehow managed to graduate on time despite it all. I was seventeen, with a narrowly received high school diploma and no clear career path. At the time, I was living in an apartment with a handful of friends while working the front desk at a local YMCA and still selling pot on the side to pay my rent. If there was ever a time to act on my future, I thought, this was it.

As luck, fate, or otherwise would have it, I received a letter in the mail from a man I now know as Uncle Bob, explaining to me that he and the rest of my father's family would like to meet me.

"I know you do not know me," he wrote, "and I know you do not know your father, but he said that just because you have no relationship with him doesn't mean you should not have a relationship with our side of the family. You've got cousins and uncles, and we would like for you to meet everybody. If you do want to meet your father, then I can arrange that."

I decided to write back, asking to be connected with my father first before venturing down to Florida.

About a month later, I received a phone call from my roommate, Doug Townsend, as I was driving. "You'll never guess who I just got off the phone with," he said.

"Who?" I asked, already feeling flush.

"Ron Poe, Jr., your father."

When he said those words, my heart leapt and I almost ran off the road. Over the next two years, my father and I exchanged dozens of calls and emails, and spent hours talking to one another online.

Then, when the timing felt right, we decided I would spend a month in Florida with him and help run a construction project he was overseeing. At the time, he was working as a superintendent building Lowe's home improvement stores. I knew nothing about heavy machinery or the construction industry, but I took any responsibility I could get very seriously. It was an opportunity, and someone taking a chance on me, a kid who few had ever taken a chance on, made me really want to deliver.

Sometimes that meant my eagerness to prove myself outweighed any insecurities and hesitations my lack of experience might have normally rendered, for better and for worse. I wasn't on the job a week before I fired one of my father's longtime workers for being half drunk and endangering the rest of the crew. Considering that my father's work revolved around a kind of "boy's club" mentality, my decision put him in a difficult spot. His crew and industry peers viewed the move as an act of disloyalty, leading to tensions between my father and me.

We tried to ease the tension one night at the giant fifth-wheel trailer my father called home. He suggested we watch a movie together, and while that may not seem like much, I had never watched a movie with my step-father, or any father figure for that matter. I was so excited to finally have that father-son experience. For years, I had been envious watching my friends with their fathers, doing normal things that Dads and their sons do together. But before the opening scene ended, my father was fast asleep, and I was crushed that this moment I had waited my whole childhood for was completely unimportant to him.

Eventually, it occurred to me that I was on the path to become just like him: a sporadically employed man among a crowd of lowlifes, all of who had begun as small-time criminals with no direction—just like me and some of my friends. He was also a terrible listener, a trait that I had often been accused of but denied. After meeting my father, I understood just how irritating it was to work with a bad listener. I decided to make a change in every way possible, and I started by getting out of Florida as quickly as I could. I remember calling my mother from the Southwest Florida airport on my journey home to thank her for not allowing my father to be in our lives.

Having met a girl at Disney World a few weeks earlier, I saw that my best chance to slip away was to join her in her native South Africa. On my flight from Johannesburg to Cape Town, I began talking to a fellow passenger about business. What began as a great conversation ended in a partnership in the very first company I ever incorporated, which we named South African Imports. Together we imported soapstone and mahogany from South Africa to Canada.

I was twenty years old and a bit unsure of what I wanted to do with my life, but for the first time ever, I had a legitimate, profitable business to call my own. Unfortunately, it didn't last long. My business partner soon vanished, and considering that South Africa was the murder capital of the world at the time, I decided to cut my losses and head back to Halifax for a fresh start in a familiar place.

When I returned, I enrolled in a local university and started training Brazilian jiu-jitsu to strengthen my combat skills. However, after just one semester at school, I was again yearning for an adventure. I wanted something challenging I hadn't done before, something that promised a larger payoff than a handful of college credits could offer me. So, I began bouncing at nightclubs to keep my adrenaline up. To make ends meet, I took a sales job for a large Canadian telecommunications company. Sales turned out to be something I was pretty good at, and before long I won a national sales contest along with my friend Andrew. To celebrate our victory, we were treated to two VIP passes to the Molson Indy in Toronto. There, Andrew and I came into contact with a large security company, and they agreed to hire us as event staff in exchange for all-access passes. At the time, I felt like I was very important—a somebody—but knowing what I know now, they were probably just short on people.

You would be right to assume that giving two twenty-year-olds—still riding high on their first performance bonus—all-access passes to the Molson Indy would be an explosive cocktail. After working security during the day, Andrew and I were invited to one of the performers' tents, where we found ourselves hanging out with a few members of the Backstreet Boys. Keep in mind it was the late '90s, and the band was at the peak of their fame. We were enjoying ourselves and cracking jokes with some of the members when we noticed two very attractive women inside the tent. We jokingly commented that we were working security for the Backstreet Boys, trying to vainly get their attention before giving up and heading over to the minibar to grab a drink. When we returned, a man I'd never seen before confronted me.

"Hey, man," he said angrily. "Me and Howie have been talking to those girls all week. Now you guys come up and open your mouths and they left. Why don't you guys get the hell out of here?"

He pressed his chest against mine and a shoving match ensued; it ended with me dragging the stranger out of the tent, ready to pummel him. Within seconds, security surrounded Andrew and me, escorted us off the premises, and told us never to return. As it turns out, the man I'd attempted to beat up was none other than Mike Rapino, the president of Live Nation, one of the largest events promoters in the world.

Before we even reached our car, Andrew's phone rang. It was the president of the security company, Mike Doherty, and he was livid.

"Jesus Christ," I heard him screech into the receiver. "I have 175,000 people at this place with no trouble to date, and your friend picks a fight with the president of Live Nation!"

I felt terrible. I had let my temper get the better of me and it cost my friend and me a valuable connection within the security industry. But there was an upside: I began to wonder if I could put my scrappiness to good use. If I could harness my temper, I knew I could combine my interest and skills for being a bodyguard with my sales and marketing instincts. But considering I'd just pissed off two of the biggest companies connected to the security industry, perhaps it was too late.

I reverted to selling weed again, only this time on a larger scale, involving a more dangerous set of players. What had once been a teenager's way of making a little extra cash quickly escalated now that I was older and had more business savvy. But more money brought more people, more violence, and, of course, more police.

After narrowly missing a raid that would have put me behind bars and effectively ended any momentum I had at the time for improving my life, I cashed out. This time, I headed to South America—particularly Brazil—to escape the mess and spend more time continuing the training I had begun with Renzo Gracie in Brazilian jiu-jitsu.

I didn't have many regrets about the choices I made during those years. I did what I knew, but I didn't expect how long my drug dealer reputation would follow me. In some circles, it still does today. That showed me the power of personal branding and perception early on. Your personal brand is like your credit score. It takes a lifetime to build, but one wrong move will stick with you for a very long time.

For the next few months, I traveled around Colombia, Costa Rica, and Panama, visiting gyms and trying to figure out my next move. In my down time, I read the autobiography of notorious

English gangster Dave Courtney, in which Courtney details his idea to hire out friends as nightclub security around London. As soon as I read it, I knew I could do the same thing back in Halifax. I didn't know much at the time, but I knew the best opportunities were found in the absence of realities. With no company offering nightclub security in Halifax, and with my experience and connections, the decision seemed obvious. "I'm a good fighter," I thought. "I can read people and a room better than most—I'll do very well at that." I also knew many boxers and mixed martial artists from my time spent training at local gyms around Halifax, so I knew I had a list of well-trained contacts I could count on to hire.

Within a few weeks, I was once again back in the city I grew up in—only this time, I had a plan: assemble a crew of bouncers-for-hire, stay out of trouble, and start watching the money pour in. How hard could it be?

CHAPTER 2

FLYING BY THE SEAT OF MY PANTS

O nce I arrived back in Halifax, I went straight to work developing a business plan (some chicken scratches on the back of a napkin). At that point, I hadn't studied the market, and I certainly didn't know much about the security industry. All I knew was that I had a knack for negotiating with people and problem solving, and I could handle myself in physical altercations. I also recognized a gap in the market, as there were no companies providing nightclub security in Atlantic Canada. I knew that if I could standardize training, wrangle insurance, and assemble a top crew, we would do more than build a great company. We would create an entire industry in our region.

I quickly moved into a flat near the nightlife district that I had bought with a friend just after we turned twenty-one. We shared the property with a pair of equally young girls from Ireland, who we frequently hung out with and pondered aloud what our futures might be. One night, the four of us sat around talking and I mentioned the idea of starting my own security company. "Oh, we know someone who does that back in Ireland," one of them said. "He rents out bouncers to bars and such around town. It's called Sword Security." A light bulb went off: I needed a name.

I immediately liked the name I'd heard. But as I mentioned, I'm a bad listener at times, and the name I heard was "Source Security."

Within days I had shirts with the name written across the chest and two radios ready to go. Without really knowing it, at the age of twenty-two, I'd begun the biggest career move of my life.

We started with two nightclubs, providing regular security on weekends. By the end of the year we had grown to fifteen nightclubs, with a few dozen, great bouncers on our roster. We had a great crew back then. Everyone took the job seriously, and I was training them on everything: from spotting fake IDs and de-escalation, to restraining a combative target using Brazilian jiu-jitsu techniques. We created our own course called "Identification, Diligence, and Awareness Training," or IDAT, which became the standard for identification training in North America.

We had a great track record, too. In all the years we worked the bars and nightclubs, we never had a lawsuit. I was aware of the risks, so I worked hard to ensure I stayed very hands-on. A few guards and I would patrol our client areas with a radio, and when a fight or disturbance broke out we would rush over, break it up, and then leave until they radioed us again. We had a lot of fun, but I was out until 4 a.m. or later every night. I knew it was a tough way to build a business, and the long hours needed for the hands-on approach left me with little time to strategize our growth. We had also incurred tons of bad debt, because nightclubs sometimes struggle to pay their bills.

As I fought to control debt and exhaustion, we were hit with tragedy. Two of our employees, Jontia Whynder and Romain Provo, were killed by a drunk driver after work one Halloween night. I was very close with Jontia, having spent countless hours together traveling. He looked like Lennox Lewis but had the personality of a gentle giant. He left behind a three-month-old son named LeShawn, who's now eleven and a huge part of my life. Jontia's passing was the first time I questioned if my business had caused someone else's death, and I struggled for months with relentless guilt and depression. It was incredibly hard on the company, too. We were still small, and the guys were so emotional about the loss of their friends and coworkers that it really tested my leadership to keep everyone together.

We survived the devastation, but by the end of our first few years, I lost my focus and let my ADD get the best of me. I decided to pull myself away from Source for a little, and use what capital I could muster to start additional companies that filled other missing niches around Halifax. I opened Halifax's first "bring your own wine" restaurant, called Milano's, and Halifax's first Asian bento box restaurant, a takeout establishment I named Noodle Nook. I also decided to travel to Thailand for a month to learn more about the food and to train in Muay Thai, a style of kickboxing (I'd fought a local champion and received one of the worst poundings of my life). The trip inspired me to dip back into the imports business, and I began bringing in everything from açaí berries from Brazil to disposable breathalyzers, and also clothing, sandals, and knick knacks from Thailand for what I thought would be additional cash flow. That plan backfired and became a drain of cash flow when I couldn't sell most of what I'd imported. To this day, I have boxes of those damn sandals in my office.

I also made some money from a construction company I had cofounded with a friend, called Castone Construction, which thankfully was doing quite well at the time. But the scattered business approach left me unfocused and even more exhausted. For the better part of a decade, I focused solely on trying to get into new businesses to create opportunities for myself. It was a shotgun-spray strategy, hoping I'd hit a target eventually. I was overcompensating for a lack of dedication to Source, using my flagship business more or less as a piggy bank for these other ventures. Whatever profit I could squeeze out of the security business I spent creating a market for another business, and then I was off to something else. By that point, I had spread myself a little too thin, trying to do everything and run all these businesses myself.

While my other business ventures failed to catch on, Source was still doing alright despite my lack of attention. The only real income I was receiving at this time still came from Source, but it was sporadic, and not really a steady paycheck. The company wasn't thriving in terms of revenue or even size, but we had built a name for ourselves in Atlantic Canada as a top security company.

We accomplished this with a simple form of branding. People don't usually notice guards at shopping centers or crowded parking lots, but everyone takes note of the guards at nightclubs—to the point where many people want to get to know them personally. Having these regular bouncers wearing our logo at the majority of Halifax's most popular clubs did more for our brand recognition than any advertising campaign could have. I didn't really understand the power of getting into that side of the market or how strong of an effect that would have on our brand until later in my career, but it did wonders. As luck would have it, those shirts turned out to be one of the best investments I could have made.

Once I realized that Source really had an opportunity to grow into something big, I decided to put more effort into it. I wasn't passionate about the security industry in and of itself, but I saw a creative challenge—to find untapped opportunities within the industry that I found exciting.

Seeing as we had the nightclub market covered, I decided to steer Source toward events. Almost from the start, I realized that working events was a completely different beast to tame. Events today have a heavy police presence, lots of policy, social media, and cameras to help keep everyone in line. Fifteen years ago, events were basically thousands of usually intoxicated event-goers versus a few hundred security guards—some with experience and training, but many with neither. But I always wanted to punch above my weight, and major event security was the biggest opponent I could find.

My first battle was a contract for a Rolling Stones concert in Moncton, New Brunswick. I had a contact from Toronto, Mike Doherty, who was overseeing security, and who funny enough, was the guy who hired us six years earlier for security at the Molson Indy. As luck would have it, he didn't remember me from my altercation with Mike Rapino there. Details were slim other than that eighty-five thousand people would be partying at an outdoor Rolling Stones concert and that I would need to provide 350 guards.

Moncton is two and half hours from Halifax, and anybody in their right mind would have laughed at the idea of getting 350 guards to travel that distance to work such a huge event. But I was determined to grow the company at all costs, and that meant taking on the biggest challenges, so of course I said yes.

At the time, I was working out of a closet in a small Halifax bar called the Oasis Pub. I had one administrator and a crew of nightclub security guys. That was it. That was my entire team, and they were less than thrilled about the risks. "No, we're going for it," I told them. "We got this." They didn't exactly agree with my optimism, but despite their reservations, we managed to put together 350 people in less than two months. It was complete chaos. We didn't onboard anybody. We were asking anyone and everyone if they wanted to work that concert. If they had a pulse, they were coming to work for us. The key thing for me was hitting the number. I didn't care if the applicants could do the job or not. I thought that as long as I had a few key people, we would be okay. We had to get everyone a security license, so the paperwork was a disaster, but we somehow managed to pull it off.

Once we had assembled our ragtag crew, we rented seven buses to transport them to Moncton, each carrying fifty people. I decided to travel to Moncton first, and instructed everyone to meet and get on the buses later that morning. My heart was trying to beat out of my chest all the way to the venue. My entire career was riding on whether I could pull off this concert, and that thought was circling in my mind the entire drive.

When I arrived in Moncton, one of my crew in Halifax called me. "Man, I've got bad news," he said.

My stomach nearly fell onto the seat. "What?" I asked.

"There's only one bus full of people. The other six are empty."

I couldn't believe it. If only fifty people showed up for security, the entire concert would be canceled. I began to panic. "We're toast in the water," I thought. "We're done. We might as well just pack our bags."

I'm not religious, but I was praying that somehow, some way, security guards were going to jump out of the woods and help me. I paced around the parking lot for a few laps until I saw what might have been the closest thing to a miracle: a stream of cars with drivers wearing our security shirts. Apparently, the majority of the guards we had recruited ended up taking their own cars, since everyone was supposed to camp overnight. I don't think I have ever been more relieved than I was at that moment.

I entered the venue and got a crash course on running security for a large-scale event. The first thing I learned was about the many layers of security, and in this case, most were from different companies. There was a guy out of Montreal who brought ten of his security people down, and Mike Doherty out of Toronto with fifteen of his people. There was the Rolling Stones' security. Then there was a guy who ran the venue's beer garden who had employed a crew of ex-police officers for his security. And everyone was barking at me to get things done. Just about every aspect of security funneled to me. The amount of pressure for one day was unbelievable, but I was adamant that we rise to the occasion.

What I hadn't planned on was how many people will tell you they'll work security just for a free ticket. Some of the people we hired took their security shirt off as soon as they got into the venue and just enjoyed the concert instead of operating their post. The day consisted of sixteen hours in the hot sun, and just about every radio call started with: "Ron Lovett, there's a major problem up here. Ron Lovett, get over here immediately." The radio was going all day—fights, drunk and disorderly, fence jumpers, lost kids—you name it. I must have had forty people yelling at me nonstop.

When the Rolling Stones were preparing to go on stage, the head of the Toronto security team, Mike Doherty—the man responsible for getting me this gig in the first place—said, "Ronnie, I'm up at gate one and there's *no* security here. You're supposed to have 40 guys up here!" We had no available security anywhere, so I had no choice but to do it myself.

Before I could leave, Bob Wein, the head of Rolling Stones' security, grabbed me and said, "Ronnie, in front of the stage, we need 186 security. If they're not there before the band goes on, we're canceling the concert and you're going to go bankrupt."

I was twenty-five years old and just losing it. I couldn't believe this was happening, so I got on the radio and said to my team, "I don't know how we get them. I don't know where we get them from. Just organize 186 people and get them in front of the stage, now!"

With twenty minutes to pull this off, we were grabbing people from wherever we could find them until we had 186 people standing in front of the stage. But like the rest of the day, every time I thought we were in the clear, something even more urgent arose.

The next problem came after the Stones' security director Bob Wein said: "Ronnie, you are to stay in front of the stage. I'll be on stage left; you're on stage right. Do not move. You cannot go anywhere. I want you up here." Bob was a security tyrant, so I knew I had to obey.

But as soon as I got in front of the stage, a voice blasts through my radio: "Ronnie, this is Mike Doherty, you get your ass back here right away. We have a major, major problem." I was completely torn.

"Oh my god," I thought to myself. "Bob Wein says not to leave. Doherty says I have to get back here right away." I pondered the repercussions for a moment, then I ducked down and ran around back, hoping with my whole being that I could return before Bob noticed I was gone.

When I found Doherty, his security had two of my security guards in custody. "We found these two guys in front of the stage," they said. "One of them was smoking a joint and the other had a beer in his hand." I didn't know who these guys were, but they had our company shirt on. The only thing I knew to do was to escalate, so I grabbed one of them and backhanded him. Then I booted the other guy. Doherty's security team went from wanting to rip me a new asshole to saying, "Holy shit, he's going to kill his own people. Get him out of here!"

So, I ran back in front of the stage just in time to meet Bob Wein. I looked at him, he looked at me, and before either of us could say anything, the Stones walked onstage to the roar of the crowd.

By the end of the night, we had maybe sixty-five security personnel left. The others had all either gotten drunk or high and wandered off. Of the 350, I might have known forty of them, and we had managed to run a concert. On the outside, it went off without a hitch. There were no major problems. No one was hurt. No one died. There were no media stories. It all worked out smoothly. But internally, it was a disaster, and probably one of the most stressful times of my life. It made me question my ability as a leader and as a manager, as well as my own handling of stress.

But despite my doubts, the outward success of the event brought more concerts and festivals to our doorstep. I began to evaluate exactly what had gone wrong: communication gaps, too many companies involved, too many inexperienced staff, too much disloyalty, too little preparation. I knew I could have my own people organize it better and do a better job of executing the security, and later on, that's what we did. We didn't need oversight from Toronto or Montreal; we *were* the oversight.

In those days, there wasn't much historical data to use when planning a strategy for a particular event. The security companies didn't know. Local police agencies didn't know. The RCMP, Canada's federal police force, didn't even have operating procedures for concerts back then. There were no manuals on how to secure a concert or festival that we could study. Everything was more or less a trial by fire, so we were flying by the seat of our pants and doing the best we could with what we had. Unfortunately, that often put us in dangerous situations.

> I KNEW I COULD HAVE MY PEOPLE ORGANIZE IT BETTER AND DO A BETTER JOB OF EXECUTING THE SECURITY, AND LATER ON, THAT'S WHAT WE DID. WE DIDN'T NEED OVERSIGHT FROM TORONTO OR MONTREAL; WE *WERE* THE OVERSIGHT.

Those close calls only further motivated us to redesign the system. We quickly adapted and implemented our own procedures, processes, and communications, and it was much smoother every time around, getting incrementally better with each event. We had even acquired a few of our own security command centres. Within four or five years, we had built a name for ourselves as the go-to security company for events in Atlantic Canada. But I still wanted us to be more, I was always looking for the next opportunity to grow Source.

If the company was going to grow, I would need to get out of the trenches first. From my time spent working security at the clubs and now at events, I realized many people working outside of Source didn't have basic security training in processes like spotting fake IDs, de-escalation, and restraining—all of which was included in the IDAT program I'd created a few years earlier. I'm talking the police, the alcohol and gaming government agencies, and the average security guard. Again, when there is a gap in the market, there is promise.

My first thought was that if I could get in to train the police, then IDAT could really take off. So, I called Robin McNeil, the head of Halifax Regional Police Training at the time, and said, "Hey, Robin, it's Ron Lovett. Listen, I've got a security company and we have this course called IDAT that would be beneficial as you train new police officers. It'll train them how to spot fake IDs and many other things." I gave statistics on what was out there, but he brushed me off.

"Yeah, send me some information. I'll have a look and get back to you." We both knew he had no intention of doing that, so I turned to what would become my first real sales strategy.

I was okay at playing hard to get with girls, which seemed to work quite well for me. I thought I'd use some of the same tactics on Robin and see what would happen. I emailed him the information, then waited strategically for about two months before I called him at a time when I knew I would get his voicemail. "Hey, Robin, Ron Lovett," I said. "As per your request, I'm following up with the IDAT course. I know you wanted me to meet with you and do a live demonstration around this time. I'm sorry, but it's not a good time for me. I'll call you next Tuesday and maybe we can set something up."

Instead, I called him on Thursday after work to ensure I got his voicemail again. "Hi, Robin, Ron Lovett here. Sorry, I know I promised I'd call you on Tuesday, but I've been so busy training this course. I apologize. I'm really trying to get around to it. I know you want me to get in there to show you the demo. I promise I'll call you Monday at ten in the morning."

This went on two or three more times before, finally, I called him at a time I said I was going to call and he picked up the phone.

"Jeez," he said, "you're really hard to get in touch with."

I said, "Yeah, sorry, Robin. I'm really busy. Look, I'll work around your schedule. When can I come in and see you?"

I went in the following week and pitched him the course.

After I finished, he stared at me for a second, then shook his head and smiled. "I don't know how you got in here with this thing, but this is pretty damn good." Sure enough, he hired me on the spot to train the police.

I managed to build a brand out of IDAT over the next few months, taking the course on the road to different departments and agencies. I even taught it at the national liquor convention in Montreal a year later, making it something of the standard for ID training. Even today I teach it once or twice a year to a department or other organization.

IDAT's success also took me to festivals and large events all over Canada, where I would present the course to staff before the action started. My training schedule eventually took me to a place called

Pemberton in British Columbia for a large festival with Jay-Z, Tom Petty, and Coldplay headlining. The event was outdoors, and it was chaos again. I thought maybe I could help, so I said, "Hey, guys, do you mind if I grab a radio and hang out a little bit? This is fun. I'll just help out." I wasn't being paid to help with the festival at the time, but you could tell pretty quickly that things were out of control. I knew just how terrible that feeling was, and the leadership team was grateful for any help they could get.

I rapidly went from someone just hanging out with a radio to someone who was volunteering to handle nearly every problem that arose. I'd say, "Hey, Ron Lovett, guy from Halifax, I'll deal with that." It was a three-day festival, and after day one, people kept asking, "Who's the Ron Lovett guy who keeps sorting problems out? Who is this guy?" No one knew who I was.

From the onset of this event, we were all instructed how to deal with Hells Angels members, who frequently appeared at these types of festivals. "If you see anyone with a Hells Angels patch or anything like that, get the RCMP right away and they will deal with it. Any Hells Angels need to be dealt with by the police." On day two of the festival, I heard that two Hells Angels members were in the beer garden. Rather than getting law enforcement involved, which I was sure would only make things worse, I decided to deal with it myself.

I walked up to the members in question and discovered they were only bottom rocker vests, meaning they were not actual members of the Hells Angels club, but prospects. So, I said calmly to them, "Guys, look, I'm not from around here. I'm from Halifax, but I told the police you guys were friends of mine. You're not supposed to wear any gang-affiliated gear, but I said you guys are really reasonable and to let me deal with it before they do. If you guys could just flip those shirts inside out, you're welcome to stay, but you can't show your patches." They both thanked me and obliged.

As I walked out of the beer garden, I saw fifteen RCMP officers who had been waiting in the wings while I was talking to them. Stories started to go around soon after. In putting out the many fires all weekend, I'd built a bit of a reputation. I ended up being put in charge of security operations backstage by Jay Z's head of security. Little did I know, six years later I would become Jay Z's personal security for his cross-Canada tour.

By the end of that festival, I had gone from someone who was there to train an ID course to someone who was essentially managing security for the entire concert. Before I left, several members of the security staff approached me and offered to work for Source if we ever worked an event in British Columbia. So I did the obvious thing—or craziest thing, depending on your perspective—and opened across the country.

I know what you may be thinking. To jump from Halifax to British Columbia is a very big jump. It would be like having your home base in Maine and then opening a second location in California. People ask me all the time why I didn't expand to cities like Toronto before making such a jump, but honestly, it had everything to do with an opportunity being there. Plus, I always like to take on the hardest thing first anyway. If I can figure out the worst-case scenario, if I can get that right, then everything else gets a little easier. Taking on the toughest challenge first will make you that much better prepared for the smaller ones that are sure to follow.

That doesn't mean I always cleared the hurdles. I was still lacking focus and saying yes to everyone and everything. We even submitted a $115 million bid to provide security for the Vancouver Olympics in 2010. I knew I had very little chance of getting it, but I wanted to get my name in with the heavy hitters. And while I didn't get the Olympic contract, I did end up working several spin-off sites around the event—a series of contracts that required Source to employ roughly six hundred staff for several weeks.

Between overextending Source that year and the earlier closings of my restaurants, I had lost about $750,000. It was a scary time, financially, but I pushed through, and the company continued to grow through doubts and adversity. I was full of piss and vinegar then, saying to myself and everyone else that "I can do it. I can do it." If I knew then what I know now, I wouldn't have done half of this stuff. Then again, I can't say that I would be where I am today if I hadn't. Like so many things in life and business, ambition is a double-edged sword—it can cut down your competitors just as quickly as it can sever you in half. I can say that I have no regrets about any of it. The experience, the things I learned—they were all invaluable in growing as a person and as a business leader. At Source, we found our niche the hard way. It wasn't by following other people; it was by chasing down the biggest opportunities we could find and learning from the mistakes we made as we went along. Eventually, what we couldn't do better than everyone else, we didn't do at all. We would never know what to avoid without having steered directly into it at least once before. Too many entrepreneurs either never leave the smooth, shallow waters, or they drive full speed and stubbornly until they hit rock bottom.

We have had huge opportunities since then, once I matured enough to focus on who we were and learned to say no. In the early days, I think we were motivated by competition and fun. Personally, I got through it because I didn't know any better, and because I wanted to prove all the naysayers wrong. That has to be part of everyone's journey if they're going to be successful: going for the impossible.

When we build our first company, most of us aren't in a position to say no. It's just yes, yes, yes. We figure out how to make it work whether it's right or wrong, and if we're humble about it, we learn from it later. Unfortunately, I don't think some of us come to the realization to hit the pause button and say, "Hold on, what are we really good at here and why? Where can we absolutely beat our competition? Let's focus there." It took me ten years to get there.

Sometimes I was hitting rock bottom myself before taking the time to self-reflect, but it was critical to my ability to move forward and create something better. In 2007, when a young employee named Jack Tobin and three other security guards were stabbed while providing security for a youth dance at the Halifax Forum. A fight had broken out, and as Jack and the others were attempting to break it up, a sixteen-year-old pulled out a knife and stabbed everyone who tried to restrain him.

I was at the movies when I got the call.

"We've got bad problems down here," one of the guards on scene said. "Guys have been stabbed and they're being taken to the hospital."

I rushed to the hospital to find the four guys all lying next to each other. I felt awful. I'd rather someone stab me than one of my guys. My company was growing and I couldn't be everywhere all the time, but I couldn't stop thinking that I should have been there. If I had been there, I thought, maybe I could've done something. Maybe it wouldn't have even happened.

Jack was in the worst condition and needed major surgery right away. Jack was a young, bright kid from Ottawa who was really nice on and off the job, and I felt especially terrible to see him in such grave condition. I gathered each of their parents' phone numbers and called them myself immediately. When I called Jack's parents, I got no answer, so I left a message. "Hi, this is Ron Lovett," I said. "Look, your son has been stabbed. You should get down to the hospital right away."

When Jack came out of the OR, the doctors told me the attacker was millimeters away from severing a major artery and killing him. They still didn't know if he was going to make it. I stayed in the waiting room the whole night, too upset to sleep. I sat alone, waiting for Jack to come out of surgery, uncertain if he would at all. Uncertainty loomed over all of us, in fact—for me, my company, and most importantly for Jack.

At 6:00 a.m., Jack awakened and began to speak. I was ecstatic, but I regretted that I had some bad news for him. "Jack," I said, "I couldn't get in touch with your parents." I didn't know anything about Jack, other than that he was a nice kid who worked hard and was incredibly humble. His parents were the only ones I hadn't gotten in touch with, so I said, "Does your mom or dad have a cell phone or something?" He gave me a number, and I stepped out of the room to call it.

"Hello, this is Brian," a voice on the other end said.

"Brian, hello. This is Ron Lovett. Your son works for me in Halifax. Look, I'm just gonna cut to the chase—Jack has been stabbed. There's been complications with the stabbing, and I think you should get yourself to Halifax as soon as possible. I'm happy to put you on a plane and put you up in a hotel. Just tell me what you need."

He said, "I'm at the airport right now. I'll be right there."

I was surprised by that. "Oh, okay."

I hadn't slept for nearly thirty-five hours. A few hours after our call, I made my way to the airport. By this time, the media began their hunt. A stabbing of this severity was a pretty big incident for a relatively small place like Halifax, but the large amount of media attention seemed strange to me at the time.

Shaking off the oddness around the situation, I picked up Brian at the airport and started the drive back to Halifax. With no small talk in sight, he immediately began asking me some very tough questions: "What happened? How did it happen? How did the kid get the knife into the dance? Do you have insurance?" I didn't know anything. I had no clue. I didn't care if I got sued. At that point, I just wanted everyone to live.

"Look, sir, we'll figure all that out. I'm sure I have coverage. If I don't, I'll pay for it myself," I said. "I don't know. Whatever I have to do."

As we were driving over the bridge to the hospital, he said half-jokingly, "Well, if this kid's lucky, he might even get choked by a former premier." A premier is the elected head of a province in Canada, and I thought, "Who says something like that? Does he have some ex-premier friend who's a fighter or something? What a strange thing to say."

I brushed it off and we pulled up to the hospital. I said, "By the way, we didn't formally meet. I'm Ron Lovett."

He looked at me and said, "Brian. Brian Tobin." He said his name very slowly, looking at me like a confused dog. So, I shook his hand. "Well, Brian, Ron Lovett. Thanks. I'll pick you up in a little bit and take you where you need to go. I'm just going to head back to the office for a second."

After he left, I called a friend. "How's everything going with Jack and his father?" he asked.

"As good as can be expected," I said. "He's a very aggressive guy, but he's nice."

"Who?" my friend asked.

"Jack's father, Brian."

"Oh no, no … Ron, tell me it is not Brian Tobin."

"Yeah, his name is Brian and his last name is Tobin."

"Ronnie, tell me Jack's father is not the Brian Tobin?"

"Who the hell is Brian Tobin?" Now I'm confused, tired, and frightened.

"He's the ex-premier of Newfoundland. He could run for prime minister."

Jack's father was a very heavy political hitter, one of the most connected in Canada, so when that news hit it was like a tsunami in the national press. I had reporters at my office, at my house—everywhere.

Things quickly escalated, and it became one of the biggest tests of my leadership up to that point. I had to do TV and radio for virtually every media outlet across the country, and then occupational health and safety came in to make sure we had all of our ducks in a row. They tore my company apart.

I felt like I was being pushed to my limit, and I had some serious doubts about whether I had what it took to keep everything together. More than once I found myself looking into the mirror and saying, "Keep going. Just keep going."

I remember being interviewed for TV and having reporters shouting questions at me. "How did a sixteen-year-old get a knife into that facility?" one of them asked.

I quickly learned to deflect: "You know what, that's a great question. But the better question, the real question, is how he got out past his probation and curfew. He was supposed to be in at 10 in the evening. This happened at 11 p.m. How did that happen?" So, I was able to bridge information to shift the focus away from Source, which turned out to be a lifesaver for both the company and me.

There were questions about our training, too. "What courses did your guys have? How prepared were they to deal with a situation like this?" Those are very dangerous questions in a situation like this, so I weighed my responses carefully. If I had said they had this course or that course, somebody somewhere was going to say, "Wrong course. They should've had this one … have had this one, should've had this, should've had that …"

So instead, I just went up ten thousand feet. "These guys are the best trained in the industry," I said. "They had more training than anybody in these types of situations." I was deflecting based on other information, which was all true and helpful to our company image. Our staff *was* the best-trained crew around, because we were the only company developing our own procedures and systems in the industry.

I was put in the fire quickly. I don't think many twenty-seven-year-old business owners have had their companies under the microscope like that, being left to deal with it head on. It was a crazy time, but in the end, we came out even stronger. Jack lived. We were cleared of any negligence or wrongdoing, and because so many people learned about how advanced our operation was in terms of standardized training, we actually walked away with a lot of positive press despite a very unfortunate set of circumstances.

CHAPTER 3

NEW TRICKS FOR OLD DOGS

R unning a business, like Source, was supposed to be easy. Following so many years of struggle, Source was finally starting to find its rhythm. We were expanding rapidly, and I was feeling more confident than ever. So, when a contract for a Bon Jovi concert in Moncton came up in 2011, the prospect of fifty-five thousand fans with 150 security guards seemed like a walk in the park. Besides, after the Rolling Stones nightmare, nothing could be much worse.

Midway through Bon Jovi's set, however, an RCMP sergeant rushed up to me and said sharply, "Ron, we have a problem." That statement is one of the last things you want to hear when surrounded by thousands of drunk concertgoers.

I took a breath. "What is it?" I asked.

"We have hundreds and hundreds of people peeing all along the fence behind the portable toilets. If you don't handle this, we're shutting the whole thing down!"

Of course, my only response was: "Okay, we got this."

In fairness, even if it wasn't our fault—the concert promoter hadn't supplied enough portable toilets—as the security provider, it was our job to solve the problem. I had to think fast. I quickly surveyed the area in question and saw that the male concertgoers were peeing on a chain-link fence standing about eight feet high. On the other side was a clearing accessible to me and my staff. So I gathered twenty security guards around me and said, "Look, I need six volunteers to come with me on a mission. We're going to go up that fence line over there on the outside of the fence, where we'll be nice and safe, and we're going to make fun of all of those exposed wieners. And I guarantee, if we do a good job at it, they will stop peeing on that fence." Lo and behold, six female guards shot their hands into the air, with one of them saying, "We would *love* to come on that mission with you." We walked up and down the fence line making fun of every size and shape we saw, and within minutes there wasn't a wiener in sight.

The security industry is very reactive, so we mostly found ourselves doing nothing more than reacting to clients' requests, no matter the urgency. A window breaks, "We need a security guard." A door doesn't work, "We need a security guard." Because clients and companies aren't as interested in being proactive, it makes for a very competitive space. Everyone is essentially doing the same thing for the same clients, at about the same price. We may have been more creative in the problem-solving process, but it was not enough to really stand apart from the competition.

In that way, we were still building a company like all the other companies. The industry was stale, and I knew it. And with Source saying "yes" all the time without innovating and my other businesses lagging, I was down to my last nickel. It was all going to implode on me if I didn't do something extreme to right the ship.

WE WERE STILL BUILDING A COMPANY LIKE ALL THE OTHER COMPANIES. THE INDUSTRY WAS STALE, AND I KNEW IT.

My firsthand experience at all levels within the industry was invaluable, but I needed to look deeper and farther, beyond my own experience. We were enjoying moments of success—whether it was winning a contract or thinking on our feet well enough to stop people from peeing on a fence—but I was beginning to feel like I was spinning my wheels. Again, I found myself growing bored and unfocused. I needed a challenge, and because it seemed like it didn't exist in my industry, I started to wonder if I should just walk away.

In hindsight, the first question responsible for inspiring and refocusing my interest on Source when I needed it most was "If I were to buy my business today, with a million dollars of my hard-earned money, what would I do differently?" I began to look at Source as a buyer would, assessing its strengths and weaknesses with as little sentimentality as possible.

At the time, we had offices across Canada, employing more than a thousand people. Some offices had several full-time, salaried employees, while others had only one or two employees who checked in occasionally. We were spread thin and were still saying yes to nearly everything that came our way. Source had no real strategy at the time. We had no alignment in our message, workforce, or workplace. I knew that if we were going to stand out, we first needed to focus on a core customer and get our management on the same page. To do that, we needed a better understanding of who we were and what we were offering to customers, as well as smarter systems in place for how management communicated with, onboarded, reviewed, and assisted team members.

The first thing I did was read Verne Harnish's *Mastering the Rockefeller Habits: What You Must Do to Increase the Value of Your Growing Firm*. Verne is an incredible businessperson who in 1987 founded the Entrepreneurs' Organization and currently serves as chair of MIT's "Birthing of Giants" leadership program and as founder and CEO of Gazelles, Inc., a planning and executive coaching company. If you haven't read *Mastering the Rockefeller Habits*, you need to right away. It is a must for any entrepreneur or business leader, in my opinion.

I'll go into greater detail about some of these systems in the coming chapters, but I'd like to introduce them to you briefly to give you a better idea of what to expect. With the advice I picked up from Verne's book, and the help I received from Gazelles coach, Andy Buyting, I began learning about company-wide systems and processes that could help fix some of our biggest problems, chief among them being how to bring together a scattered and disconnected company as it expanded. Verne and Andy first introduced me to top grading, which would become the backbone for our recruiting process, as well as for finding the gaps in our leadership and among team members. They also introduced me to the Net Promoter System (NPS) and Employee Net Promoter System (ENPS), by far the best ways to measure client satisfaction and employee engagement, respectively.

I also learned about the Brand Promise Scorecard, a system that helps define the promise of your brand. This was awesome for us, because we were able to demonstrate our brand promise before meeting with potential clients, as well as find out if our promise was measuring up to existing clients' expectations. For clients we didn't measure up well with, we had the choice of either parting ways with them or changing our approach to better accommodate their needs.

Creating new position descriptions was a great idea, too. In fact, if I hadn't started by overhauling position descriptions, I don't believe I could have pushed our HR department as far as I needed in order to grow Source. In Verne Harnish's world, a person's ability to be a "rock star" in a role requires very simple outcomes, and the ways to measure those outcomes need to be equally simple. A "rock star" is someone who takes on every function of his or her position and knocks the ball out of the park every time, so creating rock star workers is just a matter of defining their functions clearly and ensuring proper training and accountability processes for them. This created so much clarity around our expectations when hiring people that we often eliminated poor choices before they began, and it really gave the people we did hire a better sense of what their job was and how they could succeed.

Another of Verne's tips that helped us tremendously was the importance of establishing communication rhythms. As we began to spread out across the country, implementing a daily "huddle" became the cornerstone of how we communicated. We ran a call like clockwork at 1:52 p.m. AST for three and a half years. We talked about our biggest pain points, our biggest challenges or opportunities, and our biggest victories. Each huddle ran roughly four to six minutes. Our team was under pressure each day to come to the call with the most important issues that needed to be communicated. We didn't allow time to talk about whose dog got sick that weekend, or who won the latest UFC fight. Most importantly, there were no excuses when it came to missing a huddle. No meeting was ever important enough for me to miss that call. In fact, there were several calls that finished off with the sound of me flushing the toilet—it was true commitment from everyone.

For perspective, imagine a football play beginning without a huddle. Our goal was to be as well practiced as a top sports team, using the huddle as a simple check-in to ensure we were all running the same play, at the same speed, with the same goal in mind. These huddles created alignment in our management teams and fixed so many things in our business that I lost count.

With these systems in place, I began by looking at our company as a collection of people—our staff, our customers, and myself—who were all equally invested in Source. I needed to see Source as not just *my* company—which was wholly dependent on me in every department and position—but as *our* company.

CHAPTER 4

CULTURE ULCERS: THE PAIN OF DEFINING COMPANY CHARACTER

Knowing the boundaries of your brand is vital for a business leader. Understanding the limits of your product or service and those who provide it is what keeps you asking important questions before agreeing to take on a new challenge—questions like "What are the risks associated with this client? How much will those risks cost me if they occur? Are I and my team able to meet the demands in preparing for those risks?" We have all fallen victim to the temptations of shiny objects—those projects illuminated by bright lights and big paychecks—and we will all probably do it again. Taking risks and venturing into territories with a defiant ambition are all part of an entrepreneur's adventurous spirit. Asking ourselves whether we should, or even need to, rarely enters the conversation. But leading a company like an adrenaline junkie with a death wish is a sure way to doom yourself, your company, and everyone who depends on it.

I learned a similar lesson several years ago when I agreed to do personal security for Jay-Z during a few of his Canadian tour dates with Justin Timberlake. I had never met Jay-Z prior, and there was no playbook for his security detail. There was no set of dos and don'ts, what to look out for, what he likes, what he doesn't like—

nothing but a time and place to be. In the security industry, you have this metaphorical blindfold on most of the time when dealing with celebrities because every celebrity is different and comes with a variety of risks you may or may not be aware of. This can be a precarious position for new security personnel. Some celebrities may be mentally unstable and prone to violent outbursts or irrational decision making. Some may have stalkers or personal enemies. Some may be involved in illegal activity that threatens to ensnare you as well. It's dangerous taking any personal security job, especially for an A-list celebrity, where details are scarce, plans change quickly, and the general public will do anything to get to them. You have to remember that 90 percent of your time is spent being proactive, but the other 10 percent will be reactive. That can come at any moment, and in those moments, you need to move quickly and correctly or you'll be in big trouble.

In Toronto, I watched as Jay-Z ascended the stairs on the side of the stage and waited to make his entrance. I cleared the stage, making sure everyone around Jay-Z had a stage pass proving they had already progressed through the exterior security team. As soon as I swept the stage, I felt a wave ripple under my feet and shake the platform. It felt like it came from my right-hand side, so I spun around to see, but there was nothing. I looked quickly to my left and saw a large man, probably 6'3" and 240 pounds, making his way toward Jay-Z and his crew. He walked around the left-hand side of me and started walking up the stairs to an elevated platform where Jay-Z was standing. He had passed by me so quickly that I couldn't see the front of his chest to determine if he had the pass on or not.

So, I instinctively grabbed his arm and said, "Hey!"

The guy looked at me like I was out of my mind. He seemed very confident, as though he couldn't believe I had put my hand on him. "Maybe it's his cousin or a friend," I thought, so I let go and looked to read Jay-Z's body language. Jay-Z was looking at the guy the same way I had, with confusion and concern. Standing beside Jay-Z was his road manager, who was wide-eyed and jaw-dropped.

I knew then that the man wasn't supposed to be there, so I quickly grabbed him and began wrestling him to the back of the stage. We fought for a few seconds as I attempted to drag him away from Jay-Z. I eventually managed to secure a jiu-jitsu hold on him and led him down a ramp away from the stage, where I threw him off the stage and radioed for police and extra security to get him. I ran back up the ramp to make sure I was close to Jay-Z, and as soon as I made eye contact with him, I could see that he was unnerved. He was upset that the guy got on stage, and he had no idea what he might have done had he reached him.

It turned out that the intruder had snuck through the local security guards by posing as a member of the catering crew. Once he got into the backstage area, he had jumped onto an eighteen-wheeler, hopped onto another eighteen-wheeler, and then jumped down onto the back of the stage.

Jay-Z was understandably upset. "What the hell, man? What kind of security is this?" he said before walking onto the stage to perform.

As I played the event out in my mind afterward, I thought, "Here I am, making a decent wage to look after Jay-Z, but if this guy had gotten his hands on him I would have been sued into oblivion." Honestly, I risked everything to look after a celebrity who didn't know me from a hole in the wall. It was clearer than ever that we needed to think long and hard about how our core customer was, and be true to that.

Our company's new direction and the creation of our own Brand Promise Scorecard and NPS system provided a filter to help us discover our strongest client base, giving us a clearer image of client needs and problems, as well as the solutions. It was clearer than ever that we could no longer commit to these one-off opportunities—they were a distraction and began to hinder how we would start to scale business. What we needed to understand better was the financial breakdown of our current client base. After looking at the numbers, we had to brace for impact. *Roughly 55 percent of our client base accounted for 1 percent of our total revenue.* You read that right. Essentially half of our time was dedicated to a group of clients who represented under 1 percent of our total revenue. Those contracts averaged less than $1,000 each in revenue. If we were going to focus on key clients, we would have to "fire" more than 250 of our smaller clients who were classified as "reactive," meaning they initiated short-term requests to respond to a specific, often temporary concern, such as a break-in or a one-time event that required security. Our new core customer would be those in need of a long-term contract and 24/7 security.

Not only were these larger clients more profitable, they were also more predictable. We knew when our people had to be there, and we were able to proactively plan our operations around them. Our guards could build a better rapport with the client if they spent more time working with them, effectively ending the need to have a manager creating new strategies for a rotating list of small, short-term engagements.

COMMUNICATING WITH THE STAFF

It was midmorning, just a week or so after we announced, across all levels of the company, Source's new direction: to focus on a new customer whereby we were no longer reactive to short-term business. We would focus on sustainable, long-term customers who required at least one security officer around the clock, seven days a week. That, of course, meant that we had to shed a lot of our client roster by way of the biggest curse word in customer service: *no*. It also meant upsetting many of our managers, who were both fearful of the impacts their changing roles would have and frustrated by the loss of clients.

I was alone in my office when the phone rang. "Ron, this is Peter from Vancouver." His voice was tense, but sure. "I joined this company because we said if someone calls us, we would be there for them no matter what. That's what Source Security does. We take care of our customers no matter what. I don't know if that's true anymore." Peter was one of several team members who wanted me to know that their passion was to help everybody all the time. These team members were unhappy with our decision to cut loose so many small clients.

I felt bad for Peter. He had been with us for a few years, and he was one of our best staff members in the Vancouver office. Smart, dedicated, dependable—he was everything you wanted in a guard. But I had to stand firm. "That's not what we do anymore," I told him. "There's a reason for that, too. I'm going to walk you through it and tell you how we got there. And if you do not like the new direction we're headed, there are plenty of companies out there that will do the same work we used to do. I'm happy to introduce you if you find you can't move with us." I spent the next fifteen minutes explaining to Peter the reasons behind the changes in our company. I told him about the challenges to provide quality service and stay profitable, our vision for growth, our industry goals, how we would scale—everything. This was a pivot point for me as a CEO, putting an idea into action and seeing it through the growing pains. The longer you wait to pivot, the more difficult it will be when you must, especially for a large company. That is why change is so necessary in business and why you, as a leader, have to have the courage to lead through uncharted territory, even when your people begin to fight you and say it isn't going to work.

There was no playbook for what we were doing. We were the first in the industry to take such a drastic turn in our customer focus, and our people were understandably going to feel lost and maybe even skeptical

> THERE WAS NO PLAYBOOK FOR WHAT WE WERE DOING.

at first. I said roughly the same thing to each one: "I hear you. I was there, too, but let me tell you why that doesn't work. Based on this new data and information, we have to embark on a different course to achieve our ultimate goals. If you do not feel that it is the right direction for you or that we're the right company for you, I understand. And I will help you find the company that is."

Let me be clear—this communication was difficult. Many leaders decide to incite change but don't take the time to properly communicate it to the people who actually have to execute it. More often than not, when faced with any type of resistance around radical change, it becomes tempting to simply retreat. I knew there was no going back, and that these conversations needed to continue, despite the inevitable pushback from all levels of staff in the company.

Despite the sound sense it made in theory, it still wasn't easy to pull the trigger. The combination of finally doing it and losing a major client, sunk our revenues from $7.9 to $5.2 million, and for months my stomach sat wedged in my throat. I felt as though I had jumped out of an airplane with a parachute that may or may not be functional. But because we were able to focus all of our time and resources on our newly identified core customer and not be the reactive company that we had been previously, we were able to focus on systems and processes around that core customer. Meanwhile, our payroll errors and operational costs were on the decline. We had started to successfully pull Source out of a nosedive and navigate ourselves out of the fog.

Overall, our staff remained intact and more motivated than ever to rise above the norms. The combination of a series of new-and-improved internal systems and processes and the cuts we made to our client roster had our operations moving in the right direction, but I still didn't believe we had distinguished ourselves from our competitors. I began to see that the company had no alignment in its sense of purpose, because the details of who we were and what we ultimately wanted to accomplish were still largely in my head, and the uncertainty that caused was understandably scary for staff.

For us to really start focusing on our core customer, we had to further narrow our service. I knew I would have to release even more clients, and the change in cash flow enabled that move to occur sooner and with less risk. When we first began releasing clients, we started off very small–releasing those who were under about $1,000 revenue per year. Eventually, we began releasing clients that were under $20,000 per year. I also saw an opportunity to unload clients outside our desired focus while still securing some of their return. I would package those clients up, explaining to them that we no longer did this work but that we would set them up with another provider if they liked. I then went to competitors that were very small, about a tenth of our size, and said, "Hey, I've got $200,000 in revenue here that we serviced last year." These clients were not locked into a contract. They called us and we serviced them. I offered the competitor the contracts at no cost up front. I sweetened the deal even more by guaranteeing that anyone who called us fitting the same client profile would be sent to them. I would sell that to small companies by saying, "Okay, for $60,000, you make payments over the course of two years. I'll finance the whole deal. You can pay me in quarterly installments."

The deal was good for both of us, and it meant we didn't have to abandon our clients. I sold all the books of business to different competitors, but there was no real value to what I was selling. There were no locked in contracts, but I presented them as having value. The competitor could call the new company and say, "We're the new service provider." If anyone called us, we would say, "No, these guys handle it for us now. They're small and nimble, and they're focused on you as a core customer. We're not as good as them; this is a better fit for you. They'll take care of you moving forward." In the end, we were able to monetize the loss of the 250. Despite what anyone tells you, there is always a way to do a deal.

Those who worked closely with me understood exactly where we were trying to go and why, but that unified culture only existed within Source's core group in Halifax.

I got curious after the dust settled from my company's pivot in customer focus. I wondered how many leaders were directing their business the way I had for so many years, as a matter of habit or unquestioned norms. So I did some research, and what I found was that roughly 85 percent of business leaders work in their business, meaning they're going day to day trying to put out fires. Their time is mostly consumed by doing the same thing over and over just to maintain familiar, but not necessarily great, outcomes. It is the very definition of insanity: to do the same thing over and over while hoping for a different result. The other 15 percent spend the bulk of their time working on their business, meaning they stand outside of the day-to-day aspects of their business to strategize ways to prevent fires before they begin in the first place. If you can step back and steer your company strategically rather than reactively, you will do more than stimulate exponential growth in your company. You will liberate yourself. That's a process that begins by looking inward rather than upward, taking a moment to reflect on internal operations and affirm your foundational strength before the real construction begins.

I needed to hone in on my BHAG, the Big Hairy Audacious Goal, a term coined by James Collins and Jerry Porras. After visiting our offices, I began to get a sense that without having a BHAG in focus, it would be impossible for me to define company purpose and nurture the right culture to pursue it.

I was at a really low point around this time as well. Even though we had created some great systems and processes with the help of Gazelles, we were still struggling financially. It felt like we had built a great ship and were finally headed in the right general direction, but because we had no destination in sight and lacked the resources to sail aimlessly for much longer, we might just starve in the open water if we didn't catch a break soon.

That feeling was still with me when I found myself at an Entrepreneurs' Organization event in Toronto a few weeks later. The speaker was telling us about the mystery shopper programs he ran for banks. Basically, he sent mystery shoppers to open an account with a particular bank at a number of different locations. The last question they always asked the frontline staff before opening an account was "Why should I open an account at your bank versus the other five or six banks nearby?"

In the client example he used, the answers his team received were completely different from teller to teller. One would answer, "Our rates are lower." Another would say, "I think we have better hours." Still another would say, "Our customer service is the best."

Not only were the answers inconsistent, but they were also totally detached from what the bank's CEO, leadership team, and major marketing campaigns were saying about why you should do business with their bank.

After telling us the story, the speaker looked at the crowd, and I caught him staring directly at me. I knew what was coming: the speaker challenge! He challenged me and everyone else to go back to our companies and ask our frontline staff why someone should do business with our company. It hit me like a shockwave. I knew there was no way in hell the answer from any frontline staff was going to be similar to mine, or each other's. But I was up for the challenge, so I flew back to Halifax on Sunday morning and immediately lined up meetings with two long-term, frontline employees, Joel Bell and Zeb Reid.

I had Joel and Zeb come into my office that same day, because I knew it would have them wondering what the hell I wanted with them on a Sunday afternoon. I brought them in one by one and asked why anyone should do business with Source Security. Sure enough, I failed this test with flying colors. I can't remember what they said, but it was nowhere close to the message I was telling clients as I flew around the country explaining why they should do business with us.

I decided to go further with my questioning and asked them some general things about the company. Every question I asked was like another slap to the face. They didn't know we had offices in Ontario and BC. They didn't know we would be involved in the Olympics in Vancouver. They knew almost nothing about the company outside of their daily functions. I was really embarrassed, but my BHAG was suddenly in focus: *create true stakeholders at all levels*. If I could do that, I believed I could not just change my company, but perhaps the industry as a whole.

First, I had to get the message aligned about why people should do business with our company. No matter where they were in the company, everyone would know what we were trying to accomplish and how they could help at all times. We were in Toronto, Vancouver, and several other cities and provinces across the country. In all of those places, Source wasn't the same company culturally. The culture in Vancouver, for example, was different from the culture in Halifax, a disparity that emerged due to the inevitable differences between the clients, the people we hired, and the managers within that region. In fact, the lack of cultural alignment was so bad in some cases that you would have thought you were in different companies, depending on which provincial office you visited.

I had to take a step back and strategize. I began reading the book *Nuts!: Southwest Airlines' Crazy Recipe for Business and Personal Success,* by Kevin and Jackie Freiberg. The book traces the life and career of Southwest Airlines cofounder and former CEO Herb Kelleher, a fun-loving, self-made billionaire known for thinking wildly outside the box. I remember getting to the point in the book when Delta Airlines dropped their prices and Kelleher sent a memo to the entire company saying, "We are at war with Delta Airlines." The next day, the pilots, baggage handlers, and frontline clerks all had war paint on. I couldn't believe it.

As fate or coincidence would have it, I flew home for the first time in my life on Southwest—while still reading *Nuts.* I flew through New York, and as I approached the terminal counter, I put the book behind my back and said to the clerk, "Hey, I've got a question for you."

He looked perplexed, but he said politely, "What's that?"

I leaned onto the counter. "Do you like the company you work for?"

His brow furrowed and his mouth slowly drew open. "Um … what?" he asked nervously.

"The company, Southwest Airlines—do you like working for them?"

He stood up straight. "Let me make something very clear to you. *This is the best goddamn company to work for on the planet.*"

I was stunned, but sold. For an employee of a major airline to feel both that proud and that liberated, I knew the story wasn't bullshit. I also knew I needed to define and implement our culture across the country, and fast.

I went back to Halifax and started creating our core values, things that would align our company both in the way we operated internally and the messages we projected externally. I came up with three core values.

I later refined these points to create our official core values:

Teamwork

- We foster a culture of accountability, support, and loyalty.

- We always have each other's backs and coach each other to improve.

- We focus on the "Why" when we communicate.

- We celebrate each other's successes and have fun.

Honesty and Integrity

- We take responsibility and own it.

- We are totally transparent, ethical, and professional.

Continuous Improvement

- We are driven to embrace change and fearlessly seek creative solutions because of curiosity and competitiveness.

- We aren't afraid to challenge each other and address issues at the source.

I knew that if I could get everyone to look after the business based on these values, which I had never identified but had always kept in my head, everyone would have my back, because we would all be beating the same drum. I knew if I got people in Vancouver, Toronto, and everywhere else focused on managing the business by the same values we led by in Halifax, then we would be aligned in every way.

We still had management problems, however, and chief among them was our effectiveness at managing people across the country who were working at someone else's location under someone else's hours and rules. We had a COO at the time who wanted to implement a very stringent valuation system in which everyone in the company would fill out a self-evaluation and then their supervisor would evaluate them. I could not see how this system would work as the company grew. Our people were paid hourly. They did not have time to fill out evaluations on themselves, and even if they did, collecting them, storing them, and analyzing them would be expensive and time consuming. Plus, and perhaps above all, who would really evaluate themselves fairly and accurately?

To combat these blind spots, we implemented top grading. Every quarter, every employee in the country would be "top graded" on a scale from one to ten by his or her supervisor, who marked their production level, how well they did their job, and how they lined up culturally (based on our core values). Then the supervisor would answer two questions: "Would you be excited to rehire that individual based on what you know about them today?" and "Who's on your bench?" I would tell our supervisors, "If you have to let someone go, do you have someone on your virtual bench that you have developed a relationship with and feel comfortable sliding into the position?"

Once we had the marks from the area supervisors, we grouped the workers into categories. If you were a nine or ten, for example, you were an A-player. If your score was a seven or eight, you were a B. If you were six or below, you were a C. The score always went to the lowest common denominator, so if you were a seven in productivity and a six in culture, you were a six. The mandate was that the company had exactly one quarter to coach C-players up to a B or an A, or else we had to remove them.

This system did a few things. It let us know in real time where A, B, and C players were. For C-players, it was the first time they were being terminated proactively. Because the security industry is reactive, a client will call and say, "I'm sick of that security guard. I have called you three times. I want them gone." That was an industry pain point.

We were able to turn the table on that reaction. Once C-players were identified, if we were not able to coach them up, they would be gone.

We would call clients and say, "We removed so-and-so."

"Why?" they would ask.

"Well, because here's their top grading score. We didn't feel they were the right fit and they're gone. We have replaced them with someone new."

"Wow. Okay. Well, great. Thanks for letting me know."

It was a big shift in the way a company in the security industry managed its staff, one that clients had never heard of before but liked. We removed someone before clients knew there was a problem, before they had to convince themselves to complain and possibly have someone put out of a job. Who wouldn't like that?

Identifying the A-players, on the other hand, let us know who the next supervisors were. Overall, the top grading system served as a kind of engine for developing our workforce internally. It allowed us to see the "farm team" or minor leagues of a franchise so we knew where our gaps and strengths were, who was coming up or going down, and who was ready for a new leadership role.

Every quarter, A-players would receive a call from either myself or someone in HR. When I called them, I would say, "This is Ron Lovett." I typically hadn't met them before, but they knew who I was. "I just want to let you know we looked at your top grading score and you are an A-player. You line up very well with our values, and your productivity has been great. We're very excited to have you. Thank you so much for your hard work. Have a nice day!"

When someone in Vancouver got a call from someone in Halifax telling them "you're a rock star," it was like a tsunami hit the industry. This never happened. People will do just about anything to be acknowledged in our space, because too often they are seen as a number and nothing more.

We started hiring people who understood and exhibited our core values. This allowed everyone to know what would be expected of them, from applicants and new hires to our top managers. Anyone who didn't feel that our values matched their own was free to go.

The next thing we had to figure out was how we would communicate our values to existing staff. It was an important first step to get the culture aligned through the hiring pipeline, but how could we communicate what was going on to everyone else? If you do not already know this, I'm sorry to be the one to tell you, but most employees do not read the company newsletter you're emailing every few weeks. I knew that, so communicating something important would need another vehicle. We decided that our values would inform our goals and decisions at every quarterly planning session, starting with our very first one … ever. For the first several years of Source's existence, we didn't hold quarterly planning meetings, which seems crazy to me now.

At the time, our goal was to grow the business by one million dollars the next quarter. It was a lofty goal, especially with only four people planning: my COO, one regional manager, a head sales person, and me. That was it. But why would a security guard care that we wanted to grow the business by a million dollars in new revenue? A full-time or part-time guard, whether in our own backyard or across the country, would not care about this goal. So, our next mission was figuring out a way to get them more invested and aligned with the company goal.

The first step we took was to implement a theme. At the time, we had just begun using Verne Harnish's executive coaching program. We had never had a growth coach before, and looking back, it was incredibly stupid not to. Imagine an Olympic athlete trying to get better without a coach of any kind. It just doesn't happen. Hiring a coach was really the first step in getting the management team in sync with their goals and the strategies they would use to achieve them. It was at least the beginning of alignment. The program also suggested themes to facilitate company alignment, so we thought, "Okay, let's try it."

Our theme was "Operation Vacation," which is somewhat self-explanatory. The grand prize would be a trip for two to Mexico. If a security guard could tell us where another security guard company was working, they would get a ballot. If they could tell us the company who hired them and provide the contact details for the potential client, they would get a second ballot. The guards wrote their names on the ballots, and every two weeks we drew a name for an iPhone. If we hit our goal of $1 million in new revenue through those leads, we drew for a trip for two to Mexico. That had never been done before. Security guards rarely get a pat on the back much less a trip to Mexico, but I wanted to change that.

So off we went. I made a funny video (search for "Source Security Spy vs Spy Call to Action" on YouTube) with an Australian accent and sent out *Spy vs. Spy* t-shirts with "Operation Vacation" emblazoned across the chest. We had fun with it, but I honestly didn't know if it was going to work. Within two weeks, however, we were getting flooded with ballots. At the end of the quarter, we had 780 ballots. I was blown away by how much people got involved with what we were doing. They felt involved and acknowledged, and they loved it. They were finally part of something bigger, adding value to the company overall. We didn't hit the $1 million in new revenue that quarter (we have a slow sales cycle in our industry). We definitely had a ton of leads, though—so many, in fact, that we couldn't keep up with them.

I was so impressed that I decided to draw for the trip to Mexico anyway. A guard in Victoria won the trip, and he and a friend went a few weeks later. But the interesting thing about this whole experience happened six months later, when I heard that a staff member out west was upset over some issue I hadn't been aware of and was planning to take us to the Labor Board. I said, "Who is this?" They sent me the name, and it was the same person who went to Mexico. I was shocked, so I immediately picked up the phone and called him. I thought we had totally failed. As much as I thought the rewards idea was a great thing, I was now thinking, "If the guy who went to Mexico is taking us to the Labor Board, this is not working. Maybe it's a total waste of time."

When I got him on the phone, I told him who I was and got right to the point. "Look, I get that there's an issue. We'll sort it out.

Forget the Labor Board. You and I will figure this out. We'll make it right. But didn't you go to Mexico?"

"Yeah, I did," he said.

"Did you have fun?" I asked, stunned and confused.

He said, "Yeah, I did, but actually, that was the worst thing that's ever happened to me financially."

I said, "What do you mean?" I thought to myself, how the hell could a free trip possibly be the worst financial thing to happen to someone?

"First, I couldn't afford a passport. I had to borrow money from my uncle to get one. Then I had to borrow money to go on the trip. Then, when I got back, I didn't get a paycheck because I didn't work the hours. I couldn't pay my rent, so I got kicked out of my apartment."

My jaw dropped. "Oh my God, we missed it," I thought. "Here we are, a bunch of people who think we're so smart planning outcomes for individuals when we never even asked them if it was what they wanted. How dare we!"

We never made that mistake again. We always went to our people and asked, "For this next theme, what do you want? What would make you happy?" The answer almost every time was, "Give us some paid vacation." Guards never get paid vacation, and that's what we did for the rest of the themes. Communication, we learned, is very much a two-way street.

From that experience, I learned that you should always be hands-on as a CEO. You should try to touch and feel, every major decision and its impacts. Every time you make a shift in your business, taste it, touch it, feel it—look under every rock to see what the results were, and take the time to figure out the "why" behind them. You want to know if it worked, or why it didn't and how it could potentially be better. I was always hands-on. I didn't have someone else ask an employee what happened—I would have never gotten the right information. Instead, I went straight to the source (pardon the pun) and asked them directly.

The second thing I learned from the Mexico vacation prize was that making decisions without appropriate input can easily backfire, even when your intentions are completely noble. How could we make vacation decisions for people we didn't even ask? Looking back, I think we were ignorant in our thought process.

Next, we needed an all-hands-on-deck approach to push out our values across the country. We launched our "Catch the Core" quarterly theme, asking staff to take photos of themselves holding a sign with one of our core values written on it—whichever one spoke to them the most. We would post them on our social media accounts. The results were unreal. Our staff had fun with each other, as employees from all across the country found a virtual community within the company by making signs and costumes together to share with their coworkers. It was great for lifting morale and enthusiasm around the company, but even better, it helped us get to know one another in a different way. The campaign went viral within the company, and for the first time, we could physically see how we all shared and appreciated the same values. This became a really powerful visual not just for recruiting new staff but also in meeting clients, as we could visually show them our culture, not just talk about it.

Having identified and communicated our values, we decided the next thing we needed was a battle cry, something that could unite us under a common purpose. The tagline "We got this" was born shortly after. It wasn't powerful—that I will admit—but it was different. Our old tagline had been something like "Securing today. Protecting tomorrow," which is as generic as it gets within the security industry. Everyone seemed to have goofy taglines that were just horrible like that, and we were no different. It was my friend Phil Otto and his company, Revolve, that came up with "We got this" as a tagline, and at first I was hesitant about using it. I changed my mind, however, during a sales presentation with one of our sales associates. Just before exiting the elevator to meet our potential client, I said to my guy, "We got this." He turned to me smiling and said, "You just used the tagline." I realized then that I had been saying the phrase to my staff, and myself, for years, so maybe it was meant to be. The motto stuck, and for the first time, the real vision I'd had for a company since I was a teenager seemed to be taking shape. Security could be edgy, modern, and fun, and something as small as a short, punchy and memorable tagline signaled that Source would prove it.

PRACTICE WHAT YOU PREACH

Once I identified the kind of company I wanted to own, the kind of people I wanted to work with, and the values that would drive the outcomes our customers wanted, I had to do a lot of honest self-evaluating and shift some of my behavior. It wasn't easy. I already knew who I was and what I wanted my company to be: a reflection of my own values and aspirations. I had to open myself up to criticism, though, and reflect on my behavior to see when my decisions were on the mark, and when they were not.

Organizational culture is in place, either by design or by default. There are so many CEOs and businesses that do not have a defined culture. I'd be willing to gamble that roughly 50 percent of all businesses do not have defined values. Then there's another 40 percent, let's say, that have them but they're collecting dust: They may be listed online, written on a piece of paper once, or framed and hanging somewhere around the office. Trouble is, no one lives them. The CEO needs to live and breathe the company's values every day. Lastly, I'd wager that 10 percent or less of CEOs and businesses actually live their values every day.

From that point forward, I made it my personal mission to handwrite twenty to thirty cards every month to different employees around the country, from birthday cards, congratulatory cards of anniversaries or achievements, or even just telling them I had heard about something they had done and how it paralleled a particular value. I would say, "Based on the core value of continuous improvement, I heard you did this. I'm very impressed. Great work." I would also send personal video messages, text messages, and emails and make unexpected phone calls to staff to congratulate them on a job well done. I became fanatical about this. There was a time I accidentally wrote personalized birthday cards to former employees we had let go. This came to light after receiving a not-so-friendly thank-you email reading: "Thanks for the card, asshole. Why don't you shove it where the sun don't shine. Have a great day."

For the most part, people just wanted to be acknowledged, and I could do that with a simple note telling them that I noticed they were living our value(s) and it was very impressive. You do not need trips to Mexico to make your people feel valued. It's in the small, simple gestures of acknowledgment we can do every day that often have the largest and longest-lasting impact on people. As so many have said before, and for so many different reasons: it's the little things that count.

When we started to manage through our values and achieved full alignment with those values throughout the company, it was more powerful than labor standards. Before, we were taken to the Labor Board somewhat frequently, but in the four years since Source began managing through its values, we did not go once, despite having doubled in size. I attribute that almost exclusively to our decision to confront ourselves and define, and adhere to, a common value system.

Now that we had defined our core customer, and our values were intact, I was hoping that would be enough. Unfortunately, we had only just begun.

FIGHT TO THE FINISH

CHAPTER 5

FIND, SHIFT, ALIGN:
A RECIPE FOR SUCCESS

As soon as things started to look up, I was dealt another blow when Jodi, our HR star, decided to leave the company. It was a particularly difficult decision to hear, because Jodi had been with Source almost since the beginning. She loved the company and loved our culture. I was really starting to push her and get her out of her comfort zone so she could add real value to the company. At one point I told her, "Jodi, if you're not willing to challenge things I say, then I don't need you here. If you're a yes-person, then you do me no good. I'm not asking you to fall in line. I'm not asking you to be a jerk, either, but I do need you to challenge things I put forward. That's your job, to collaborate with me."

Jodi really came out of her shell after that, so much so that she decided to pursue a position with a startup. They had asked her to open an HR consulting division, one that she could build as her own. She was excited and asked if we could talk about it. She told me about the offer, and I knew immediately what I had to do. My job as a leader is to get everyone in my care to their own personal goals, not my own. I can't let my own ego get in the way and say that everything and everyone has to be about the company or me. It's about the individuals that make up a company, after all. I can push them to be their best internally, but if their best means going outside of my company, then that's my job, too. So, I said, "Jodi, go for it. I support you. Life is about new challenges, new risks. You should take this opportunity."

With that, off she went. Within two or three months, however, she called and asked if we could have coffee. I said, "Of course." So, we had a chat, and she began telling me about some of her challenges at the new job.

We were brainstorming about how she could get around them when she said, "I really miss this."

I said, "What's that?"

"Here I am coming to you about challenges in the new business I'm in, and these people aren't willing to have these conversations with me. I kind of feel like I'm on my own. Even though it's a startup, we don't have the openness that we had here. We're not really a team, and we're not collaborating on stuff."

I said, "That's too bad. Wait it out and see if it improves."

Sure enough, within nine months she called me and said, "Ron, I'd really like to come back."

Part of me felt disappointed for her that it didn't work out. The other part of me, however, couldn't help but enjoy knowing Source had the unique culture the small startup was supposed to have. It was our culture that brought Jodi back, and it was positive proof of just how powerful it was.

It's like they say, you don't know what you have until you lose it. I think Jodi saw the power of our culture once she stepped out of it. It was a norm to her on a day-to-day basis, until she went to a different norm and said, "Wow, this isn't what I'm used to and it isn't what I really enjoy." She did come back to Source, and we welcomed her with open arms. Jodi became an example to others that I would support them in new challenges if it's what they wanted, but our culture was so strong that they may want to return regardless.

When you look at companies with strong cultures, you find organizations that articulate who they are and what they do and what they expect of employees through a very specific and simple purpose. Google's mission, for example, is to "organize the world's information and make it universally accessible and useful." Starbucks says its purpose is to "inspire and nurture the human spirit—one person, one cup, and one neighborhood at a time," while Disney simply wants to "make people happy." These are large companies that have managed to achieve outstanding profits for many years while simultaneously changing their respective industries and maintaining a productive workplace with a comparatively satisfied workforce.

I was still contemplating how those companies got there, but I knew I needed to simplify our purpose and stick to what we did best. People need to know why their work is important, and the only way to find that answer is by understanding how one's work is connected to something larger than the job itself. When I think about purpose now, I'm always reminded of a story a friend told me about Steve Jobs when he courted then Pepsi president, John Sculley. Whether the exact words were said, I can't be sure, but allegedly, Jobs sat Sculley down and said, "Look, I've got this company, Apple, and you should come work for us."

> PEOPLE NEED TO KNOW WHY THEIR WORK IS IMPORTANT, AND THE ONLY WAY TO FIND THAT ANSWER IS BY UNDERSTANDING HOW ONE'S WORK IS CONNECTED TO SOMETHING LARGER THAN THE JOB ITSELF.

Sculley said, "I work for the second largest company in the world. Why would I ever want to come work for Apple?"

Jobs's response was bold: "Why? Because we're putting a dent in the universe. If you'd like to be a part of that, this is the place to do it. Or do you want to keep selling sugar water to people?" Sculley joined Apple the same year.

That story really stuck with me, swirling around in my mind as I said, again and again: "We need to have a purpose that will align us with what we're really doing here. What are we doing every day? What are the values guiding how we do it? Why are we here?" I spent several weeks thinking about those questions, and the answers always came back to the idea of changing the industry. Purpose has to be powerful enough to make the hair stand up on your arms. Has to be powerful enough to be a conversation starter. It has to be powerful enough to hold people accountable to it.

Then it became obvious. Our purpose was to change this industry, which would accomplish all three. We hated the industry how it was. We worked in it every day and yet we hated what it had done to the employees. We hated that the clients were so under-served. We hated the outdated model that dominated our industry. We needed to change the industry if we were going to take Source and its new vision to the top. That realization was a defining moment in our business, because it gave us unity. Once we started to push it out, we had everyone beating the same drum in terms of why we went to work.

Purpose became such a priority that we hired people by telling them that they were joining us to change the industry. We then said, "Tell us how you can help us change the industry." If a current employee presented me with a system or a process, I would say, "Does the industry currently do that? If so, throw it out—we don't want it." If I was at a trade show and a salesperson came up to me telling me about some new software that "the biggest companies in the world use," my response was the same every time, "If it's already being used by the industry, I have to find something else." It would drive people crazy, but it made things incredibly clear for us. We had to be the first. Always.

That idea eventually became our elevator pitch. A client would ask the question they all love so much: "What makes you different than your competition?" We used to be like every other unfocused company and give the generic answer: "Our training is a little better. We hire great people. Our equipment is a little better. Our vehicles are a little nicer." It's the same bullshit every time.

When we started to ask ourselves what *really* made us different, we came up with a much simpler, more intriguing answer: "We have a purpose to change the industry." No one could challenge us on that. They would just say, "Oh, wow, that's really different. Okay." Once their interest was piqued, we would explain more about how we were changing the industry. That one sentence became our sales pitch. It intrigued people and drew them in, until they were interviewing us. The old outward pitch had left us chasing bored clients and trying to sell them on services and clichéd promises that a dozen others had already offered them. We wanted the right clients, and we found them by being bold and clear about our core purpose. An inward pitch, one that tells the listener something interesting and inspiring, brings them into our world, because they want to know more. Once they do, we're not so much selling them as we are showing them under the hood, so to speak, and letting them know how our company is changing the industry. That's exciting for both the potential client and our sales team. You can't get better alignment than that.

Once our purpose was defined, I needed to take a step back to get a broader perspective. I went back to the drawing board by asking myself yet another pivotal question: how could we truly operate differently? "What if I had to restart the *industry* today? Knowing what I know now about the internal and external challenges—and using the technology and resources I have available today—how would I create a new model to overcome those challenges while maintaining industry average or above profitability, in which everyone could be a leader, a decision maker, and an innovator?" When I did, I uncovered a lot of things that we needed to change. First, there was poor morale among guards and a high turnover rate industry-wide. That stemmed from the long hours, limited flexibility, lack of transparency, poor benefits, low pay, and staff being constrained by too much policy—all major points of the entire industry. The staff that did stay were typically just comfortable at a specific client site, which had nothing to do with the company that hired them. Alternatively, they simply lacked any other options. Poor customer service and work quality ensued, and companies across our industry had imposed even more policies and bureaucratic hierarchies in an effort to improve it. If I could change all of that, then I would be more than a few steps ahead of the competition. It would require a drastic change, of course, as our entire business model would have to be redesigned.

I wanted to look outside of what was a stagnant industry to find new ideas that might help us, so I continued to study companies like Google, Starbucks, and Southwest Airlines for pointers on strategy and execution.

A company that stood out above the rest was Uber, a private transportation service. Uber's success was almost instantaneous, because they took a stale, sleepy industry (like ours) and defined all of the customer pain points that made traveling from A to Z a complete nightmare, eliminated them, and built a win-win model easily executed for both passengers and drivers. When I began diving into Uber's strategy, my first response was "How in the world did these generational taxi companies, as the masters in their industry, not identify what Uber saw?" That was not going to be me.

Similar to Uber, we had exceptional challenges around industry standards. For one, security is largely a minimum wage industry. That was perhaps our greatest challenge: getting people who earn so little to care so much. In truth, most security companies, and even some of our own clients, treat guards like second-class citizens. This fueled my Big Hairy Audacious Goal (BHAG) of transforming the industry by turning a disgruntled staff into passionate stakeholders who were all synchronized with our purpose and vision. Everyone said it could not be done due to industry commoditization causing barriers, the custom of managing through a rigid, military-like hierarchy and set of policies and procedures, and the inherently low pay. We were facing greater challenges than Southwest Airlines or Starbucks. But I accepted the challenge anyway. We immediately stopped using the word "employee," replacing it with "staff," "stakeholder," or "team member."

Another major challenge was that we were relatively disconnected from most of our team members. Most of our guards didn't come to our office every day. I didn't meet them before they were hired. They weren't coming to company parties and team-building events. We shipped them a uniform and paid them by direct deposit, and they worked at someone else's location. If we were Starbucks, let's say, the employee would show up to work in our environment, led by our values, and there would be a manager to assist and assess the employee at all times. In contrast, our staff showed up to a shift at a client's place of business and had to perform under that client's culture. The guards rarely even worked with one another. One showed up for his or her shift as the other's shift was ending, and aside from a brief rundown of events or instructions, there was no interaction between them. I knew they didn't feel a sense of community by working under our brand.

What if we gave the same level of management autonomy to our frontline staff? It was time to have another coffee with Joel Bell and Zeb Reid to test my theory. Sure enough, when asked if they would like to make the decisions their managers were making for them today, they were both excited and up for the challenge, even without mention of a pay raise.

Then it became clear: it was time to give employees their brains back, and time to restructure management. Our frontline security supervisors who were doing laps, checking doors, and writing reports at the shopping center and hospitals were now in a position to act like managers in a multi-million dollar company. You read that right: these minimum-wage workers were now given as much or more autonomy than their old operations and regional managers combined—positions that were now completely eliminated.

We were taking a big risk by making good on our cultural changes, and I remember this period in our evolution as being very stressful. I was personally removing midlevel managers I had known for years, people who had been with me since the beginning but who no longer agreed with me on our new values and/or direction. It was time to give our frontline staff a sense of purpose. I wanted to let them manage the functions that midlevel managers were always overwhelmed with and couldn't execute properly. Again, a fresh vision often means fresh people. Some will stay on and adapt. Some will not be willing to make the effort and will drop off on their own. Some will actually thrive because of the changes. And, as hard as it is, some of your best and most loyal employees either will no longer fit into the new model or will not share the same enthusiasm for your new direction, and conflict will arise.

Change is never easy, for anyone. Redesigning commonly held business and personal beliefs was not easy for us; nor should you think that doing such a thing will be easy for you. But as the common expression goes, if you don't like change, you are going to like irrelevancy even less. Unfortunately, change will always be harder for those most familiar with what's being replaced, and for many of our veteran managers, ripping up the old management ways was just too much to adjust to so late in their careers.

But knowing that what you're trying to build will open doors you never knew existed gives you the will to do just about anything. Because we were changing so drastically, employees who were only partially dedicated to the company to begin with were the first to jump ship. Once our mission was clear, I knew exactly who we needed and who we didn't. The clarity and brazen approach to challenging our industry's model meant that I could recruit the right people simply by selling them on our vision of being the best. We were not willing to accept the norm, and we expected that our staff not accept it either.

In moving away from a thick, midlevel management model, I anticipated having a large number of exits. But I wasn't so sure how we would be impacted, and that was an admittedly terrifying reality to consider at the time. What gave me comfort was the belief that if we could align the workforce with a sense of purpose and culture, then our management systems would simply have to wrap around them to hold on to the people we most wanted. In other words, our company purpose and culture would serve as a workforce filter. For that to happen, however, we had to communicate our values clearly. We knew the first step toward creating the kind of trust necessary for such an immense change was being honest with our people. That meant we had to address the elephants in the room by talking about uncomfortable issues such as low pay, internal distrust, and our lack of cohesion. We wanted to lay a foundational belief that solving problems meant open communication. People will not communicate openly and honestly if they do not feel safe, which was already an industry-wide problem in our case.

From that point on, we were more transparent about our decisions and goals, and in turn our staff became enthusiastic about getting involved in the problem-solving process. They felt more comfortable sharing their ideas and concerns, which allowed us to give them more of what they wanted and needed. In essence, our people felt more important, and when people feel important to their company, they are more invested in their jobs. When your people are happy, challenged, and stimulated, your organization is firing on all cylinders. With a team like that behind you, the sky is the only limit for what you can achieve.

Once we created our new model, we were entering uncharted territory, which was scary for my staff. To be honest, it was terrifying for me as well. Out of all the books I had read and all the seminars and conferences I had attended, no one ever talked about how to operate within such a model.

We went from fourteen regional operations managers, four regional directors, and a COO to a handful of HR staff, salespeople, and a few accountants.

As you can imagine, in our business, the key issues around HR are mainly ensuring that guards are showing up for work on time, hiring guards for sites, and dealing with client issues as they arise. With our new model, we were pushing these responsibilities down to the site-level coordinators or supervisors. The question became "Who do they go to when they're stuck or in need of support?" At the time, they were randomly calling different people from HR, sales, and finance to help with issues on the site.

To remedy the problem, I came up with an idea for what we called the "company support map." The interesting thing to point out here was that this was the first time I took a large idea to my frontline staff first, rather than my management team. I spent countless hours meeting with them and discussing my vision for a company map they could access on their computers. Essentially, the map would tell everyone who they would contact in the company for critical issues, as well as provide a link to a system for that issue. So, if the issue was related to getting their expenses covered, the company map would point them to the controller, give his contact information, and connect them to a link where they could fill out an expense report.

It was very eye opening to go through this process with my frontline staff first, because they found the gaps in the process. I finally had 100 percent buy-in because they helped to create it. Only after I had workshopped the idea with the front lines did I bring it back to my management team to tighten up. When it was all said and done, it worked wonderfully. Everyone felt supported and knew exactly who to go to for a specific issue or had links available to them that provided information on how to deal with a particular issue.

They could go directly to HR, finance, or client services if they had a problem, but they couldn't reach out to a broader source of help across the company. They were not able to build many relationships, because they only knew one or two people outside of their frontline team. We decided to fix that problem by giving them direct access to all their peers across the country.

We changed their titles to site coordinators, which was more of a midlevel operations or HR manager title, since our frontline people were now doing the functions of midlevel management.

Let's be clear—these day-to-day challenges our people supported each other through could never have been resolved simply by adding more managers. We knew through experience that more managers equalled more bureaucracy, slowed efficiencies, and depleted morale. On top of all of that, in a thin-margin industry, adding management meant the frontline guards suffered in regards to personal compensation. By introducing our new model, problems were being solved faster and cross-departmental relationships were being formed. We were starting to build a real community, which had long been missing—not just at Source, but within the industry.

Now that we were trusting our frontline people to step up, I started to see some incredible things happen. We had better engagement, increased productivity, and happier clients, and we were doing it all while shrinking our costs. If this was a cultural side effect, then I knew we had to spread it.

As a company, we had a new soul. We knew our core values. We understood the kind of culture we wanted to create, and we had a simple tagline that reminded everyone of its essence every day. We had an ultimate purpose behind our daily work, providing us with clear parameters as we drove toward a shared goal and we finally had a new operating model.

For me personally, I was starting to figure out that the better I was at staying true to myself and keeping things simple, the happier and more productive my employees were. That emanated through the company in such a way that clients were drawn to us on their own. I had always believed that if I could build something great the hard way, everything else would be easy (I learned later that it wasn't *easy* so much as it was *easier*, but *easier* is generally all you can hope for in business). That belief was beginning to be realized. Plus, the straight-forward, fun, and competitive nature the new direction fostered was a welcome refreshment. Life and work felt more natural around the office, with everyone working in rhythm and feeling more confident in their efforts. From top to bottom, the staff was now involved in the bigger purpose of the company, which in turn gave their work a greater sense of personal purpose and pride. You can't replicate the kind of motivation and dedication that stem from those feelings.

We were vulnerable with our people, saying, "Look, we know things aren't perfect. No matter where you work in this industry, things aren't going to be perfect. The pay isn't going to be great, and the work is going to be hard. We want to change that with Source, but we need your help." A-players love those kinds of moments because it's a time to shine, as well as a chance to do something different. A-players need to be challenged to maintain their interest, and they need opportunities to shine, not only for us to find them but to keep them as well. So we would go to our staff, lay out the theme of the problem, and say, "We need help with this topic. We're trying to figure out a new system for this." We were reinforcing our original idea that our people were stakeholders, not employees. They weren't just being told what to do anymore. They were helping us live our purpose, which now was never ending.

CHAPTER 6

BEAT STARBUCKS: COMPETE AGAINST THE BEST

t should not come as a shock that most business owners get into business with the aim of doing things a little better—they don't set out to do things absolutely differently. I know I didn't.

I was pitching security for ten years to people whose eyes were glazing over. Unless I could tell them about the time I spent a week working as Nicole Kidman's bodyguard or something that was half interesting, they were going to fall asleep every time. But once I got to the place where I would talk about our new model and purpose—show them under the hood, so to speak—the question I asked them every time was "Have you ever heard of anybody in the security industry that operates like this?" When the answer was invariably *no*, I knew we were onto something.

PLAYING—AND WINNING—OUTSIDE YOUR LEAGUE

Despite the changes to our company, we were still competing against big companies with deep-rooted cultures. I knew two things about that. First, the old tried-and-true type of competitor thinks they have it figured out. They're running their best version of the old model. It was very clear there were companies who ran a better version of the old model, and those were the companies we wanted to avoid competing with as much as we could. We needed to focus on the niche markets within our industry, and having a completely different model and culture would help us do just that. From our perspective, the changes in Source's purpose disarmed those companies. No one really jumped on our ship, which was as much a relief to me as it was concerning. Did they know something we didn't? I told myself they didn't. Besides, it was too late to turn back now anyway—company morale and our profits *were* rising.

The second thing I knew was that for someone to compete with us now, they would have to start from scratch and say, "That's the company I want to build." We didn't see others having the courage to go there, at least not yet.

Imagine if you had your people going back to the drawing board in everything they do, from how they onboard people to how they sell to how they engage clients to how they collect cash. If everyone is going back to the drawing board all the time, you get hyper growth and your competitors don't stand a chance. And not just in how you deliver your end service—that's just one piece of the puzzle.

Take your business apart piece by piece and examine everything you do—from how you hire and train, to how you sell and market your product or service, to what it is you do in its simplest form. By pushing your company to seek solutions creatively, you are laying a foundation on which your company can grow and repair itself over its lifetime. If you don't, then you may be brought down by a bored teenager in their parents' basement with a vivid imagination and a knack for technology.

Do not buy into the belief that to be successful you must grow up and put away your childish imagination. Tap into your childhood mind to find a world where there are no borders, no rules or status quo, just the possibilities of "what if." We have all heard the cliché "if it ain't broken, don't fix it." Why not? So many people have said that to me throughout my life, and it's never made sense. If it's not broken, I say, break it and put it back together better than the way you found it. For Source, all the breaking and deconstructing we had done to our model left us wondering one thing as we put ourselves back together: how could we push this even further?

We wanted to keep innovating to stay one step ahead just in case an industry competitor emerged. One victory essentially led us to another battle with ourselves. Every battle required us to look at how the industry did things we might be able to do better. Unfortunately, the "industry bar" was set so low that our successes along this path didn't really mean we had won the war.

A product can only be as good as your ability to provide it. You have to know what you do best and be humble enough to acknowledge what someone else does better than you, and then let go of it. Harvard professor, author, and business consultant, Frances Frei, along with co-author, Anne Morriss, proposed in their book *Uncommon Service* that companies should "dare to be bad." Take companies like Wal-Mart and Southwest Airlines. They are excellent at some things, and they're horrible at others. Wal-Mart has excellent pricing, fully stocked shelves, and the convenience of having just about everything you need in one place. But they do not have great ambiance, and they have notoriously bad customer service. Southwest Airlines has a great culture, great customer service, and great pricing, but they have horrible seat selection and no VIP lounges. Neither company pretends to be good at their weak points, but they are fanatical at understanding their core customer and they win at making sure they are the best at maintaining the attributes that are most important to their core customers. Every company has weak points. Finding out where yours are is a lot easier if you're brave enough to look.

We wanted to know what was most important to our core customer and focus on that, so we started by studying our industry's attributes. We broke them down into twelve categories—customer service, pricing, guard knowledge, mobile response, local offices, and others—and divided those into four quadrants of three. Then we went to our new, clearly-defined customers and potential customers and said, "What is most important to you?" They would list and then choose from the most important quadrant to the least important quadrant, giving us an idea of what they wanted and how we could deliver it to them.

What came out of the surveys? The number one thing for our clients was customer service. How our guards treated their customers was the top priority. I always thought it was pricing or guard knowledge, but it wasn't. The lowest attributes were things like having a local office and having mobile patrol, which is when a supervisor in a car comes out to make sure guards have their uniforms on and aren't falling asleep on the job. We drew it all up on the board and started brainstorming how we could align what we did best with what our clients wanted most.

We decided to shut all the offices down and sold seventeen patrol cars. No one cared about them, and they were costing a lot of overhead. We went digital, using technology to keep in contact with our guards and help them with their work. If we had a customer that cared about an office and cars, then we couldn't do business with them. We made a decision that we were going to be awesome at customer service and bad at having local offices and cars on the road. It drastically improved our gross profit margin, and we used the resources we saved to focus on what was important to the customer. It also forced management to go out and visit staff and clients, since they no longer had an office. Management visiting staff and clients regularly was a major industry pain point, and the change elevated our service and client relationships tenfold. One of the most common questions we got from our clients during a sales meeting was "Where is your office located?"

I was always excited to answer this question—"We purposely shut them all down. As you know, in this industry, managers often sit in the office all day answering phones and putting out fires. We want to ensure that our managers are out working with the frontline staff, ensuring client satisfaction and truly getting involved with all layers of our business."

Now that we didn't have the expense of brick-and-mortar offices all over the country, we were able to pay our people a little bit more, too. Also, we had no midlevel managers. Most companies operate at a 25 percent to 30 percent gross margin, which is then eaten up on the back end because of managers and all the infrastructure to operate. We had none of that, so we were nimbler. We were also more aligned internally, allowing us to provide better service. Without the bureaucracy, we could also provide our product for a better price. Our site level margin had decreased, but we had a healthier overall margin because our overheads were so much less. We were winning in the back end, and our revenue growth exploded as a result.

We created a chart to rank ourselves against the industry by assessing every industry attribute the same way. We drew all the attributes on a board and said, "Okay, if customer service is most important, where do we think we are on a scale of one to five?" If we thought we were a three on customer service, which happened to be most important to our customer, then we said, "Okay, who is our biggest competitor, and where do we think they are?" We found we were a point or two higher than multinational and local companies were. Conventionally, we could have stopped there and declared our victory, but we knew being a point or two higher wasn't enough to get the industry to notice. If we were going to get their attention, we had to think outside our own industry.

We said, "Okay, let's take a different perspective. If it is customer service, what business has a similar service delivery?" A lot of customer interaction, low wages, and large operating territory were among our metrics for finding a similar business. We needed fresh competition and a new insane challenge to light a fire under all of our asses, and Starbucks was the perfect target. As soon as we all agreed, I said, "Look guys, that's our competitor. Forget the other security companies. We need to go after Starbucks. If we can beat or even get close to Starbucks, then we win."

FORGET THE OTHER SECURITY COMPANIES. WE NEED TO GO AFTER STARBUCKS. IF WE CAN BEAT OR EVEN GET CLOSE TO STARBUCKS, THEN WE WIN.

I started going to Starbucks regularly, and our team began getting their drinks at Starbucks. We would talk to Starbucks managers, figure out how they hired, how they onboarded, how they trained, everything. We studied them as if they were our competitor. Around the office, the new challenge was crystal clear: beat Starbucks.

Everyone, new hires and current staff, had to watch our onboarding video, which included the standard onboarding information, such as how the company started and what our mission, values, systems, and processes were. I made it 100 percent clear that from a customer-service standpoint, we were competing with Starbucks. We needed to hire better than Starbucks. We needed to train better than Starbucks. And, perhaps most important to us, we needed to create better systems around customer service than Starbucks. Thanks to

John DiJulius' book *The Customer Service Revolution,* we decided to throw out the golden rule—we created a customer service "bill of rights" based on the platinum rule (i.e., treat people how they *want* to be treated), where our customers had a specific set of rights that were made known to them. This bill of rights would hold us accountable and inform a decision-making process for every team member, top to bottom. One of our customers' rights, for instance, was that we couldn't tell them what they couldn't do without telling them what they could do. This clear customer bill of rights allowed us to measure our staff's customer service.

We made it our mission to be the most special part of a customer's day, and that goal gave us the alignment on customer service. It changed how we delivered on our brand promise, because the ultimate purpose of our customer interaction was clear. A guard, manager, or office worker knew exactly what they were supposed to do for the customer and how they were supposed to interact with them. Of course, that meant we had to have the right people in the right positions, too. We'll talk more about that in the next chapter.

As we had already learned from our client surveys, customer service was the most important outcome for our customers. That made me think, "The number one attribute for an individual to provide great customer service is empathy." A person must care about the customer if they are going to serve them well. You can't train someone to be empathetic. That realization led us to change how we hired. We would have to screen people for empathy. From that moment on, we only hired people with the traits associated with being empathetic. This was a pivotal moment in our recruiting process. Imagine that, we now had people in a customer service role who truly cared about other people.

If you want to be the best, use your courage and creativity to enter uncharted territory and learn. You need to look at which industry attributes your core customers value the most and which ones are irrelevant to them. You need to find out how the top company on the planet executes those attributes better than anyone—don't restrict yourself to your current industry. Once you've identified those strengths, ask yourself: What programs do they use, how do they hire, how do they train, how do they market their product? What's appealing about their brand? Hold yourself to the highest standards, and while you may not be able to meet every one of them, you will always find ways to be better than you currently are. Without the excitement of progress and competition, complacency will take hold throughout the company. Before you know it, you're dead in the water with competitors on the horizon. Before you know it—you're Blockbuster.

CHAPTER 7

GIVE PEOPLE THEIR BRAINS BACK

Every time I got a little closer to our purpose of changing our industry, I asked, "What's the next level?" When we found purpose and core values, for instance, the next real challenge was moving closer to our BHAG of changing an employee to a stakeholder. The industry was so policy driven, so entrenched in rigid rules, that companies were accustomed to firing anyone who did not listen to the rules. In essence, employees were treated like children, and disposable children at that. If we were going to convert employees into stakeholders, then we had to offer even more autonomy. More autonomy demanded that we go places others were not willing to go with their business, such as dismantling management structures or abandoning a brick-and-mortar model. Once we did these things, I saw the changes internally at first. I saw the outcomes of our new model in the small moments, such as an encounter I had with a team member named Ashwani Walia.

After acquiring a customer in the trucking industry in Toronto, I decided it was an opportune time to test the theory that when people are given a great challenge, they will show up with an even greater resolve to meet it. Ashwani was the security manager at our new Toronto client location, who had been in the position under a slew of different companies for nearly fifteen years. Not long after taking over the contract, I got a call from Ashwani informing me that we needed a new truck at the location. I already knew we needed a new vehicle, so I said, "Well, Ashwani, you've been there for over ten years. What kind of vehicle do we need?"

"Uh, well, sir…it needs to be one that has four-wheel drive. It needs to have plenty of space for passengers. It needs to be safe, of course. And…" I immediately knew what needed to happen next.

"Let me stop you right there, Ashwani," I said. "It sounds like you know what we need. I tell you what, why don't you go out and find us a good deal on a new vehicle? If you do, we'll pay you a commission."

For the next few seconds, there was only silence on the line. I didn't know if I had lost him, or if he was just stunned. Finally, he stammered a bit. I realized that Ashwani had never been challenged. He had never been a part of something that allowed him to use his own ideas and make his own decisions. After a few more seconds, Ashwani said, "Sir, I will find the best vehicle for you." And he did. He got us a great deal on a new truck that we desperately needed. Of course, our controller at the time could not believe that we were allowing a frontline security guard, who was new in our company, the autonomy to go and buy a truck in Toronto. But think about it for a moment. Who is better suited to buy a truck in Toronto: an accountant here in Halifax, or an employee out to prove himself by showing that he can go to a dealership, haggle, and negotiate a good purchase for the company? The answer was very clear to me. This moment also told me, unfortunately, that our controller was not culturally aligned, or aligned with our purpose, and we would be parting ways in the near future.

Six months later, I went to Toronto and had coffee with Ashwani's former boss from G4S, which is the largest security company on the planet, operating in 187 countries with revenues of $8 billion.

"Tell me something," I said. "Did Ashwani keep his vehicle clean when you were his boss?" He shook his head fiercely.

"No. It was a total mess. We had to write him up several times because that vehicle was so messy."

Soon after, I ran into Jim Kennedy, who worked at our Halifax office and had just been at Ashwani's location, so I asked him about his vehicle. "Is it clean inside?" I said.

"Man, you could eat your breakfast off the floorboards," he said.

Right then and there, I knew we were onto something. We had converted a person who had worked for five or six different companies as a unionized, average employee into a passionate stakeholder.

Another example of this comes by the way of Paul Crawford. Paul was a guard in rural Nova Scotia who had transformed to someone who was completely invested in the success of both the company and his teammates. In the security business, when a guard gets a day off, they always take it. No question about it. But when we found ourselves short staffed and in need of someone to cover a shift, Paul stepped in to rescue the situation. Not only did Paul volunteer to cover the shift on his day off, he offered to do it on his birthday.

When I heard the story, I was so impressed by his selflessness and dedication to helping his team that I sent him an email to thank him personally.

"No problem," he wrote back. "This is my company, my family."

His response floored me. It was proof that what we were doing was working. I was so ecstatic by his attitude that I wanted to climb Mount Kilimanjaro and shout it to the world. I settled instead for a company-wide email detailing Paul's actions and words. I typed it out on a flight from Halifax to Toronto, copying Paul's words into the message while explaining how proud I was of his commitment as a stakeholder in the company. As anyone who knows me can attest, however, my typing skills are, well, subpar to say the least. Couple that with being in a rush and the phone's autocorrect, and you have the recipe for some very interesting messages.

After I sent the email to a thousand-plus staff, my assistant went straight to my wife and told her, "This is bad. He really messed up this time."

As it turns out, what I had actually written read as follows:

Date: March 20, 2016
From: Ron Lovett
To: All staff

Hey guys see Paul's email below. Very proud that we have suck dedicated and patio are people. Spoken like a true steakholder!

Ron Lovett
President, Source Security & Investigations

I don't know if people knew what I meant or not, but the actions of Paul were probably playing second fiddle to my egregious and hilarious errors.

As soon as I got home, my wife said, "Sit down; we are going to talk. You are the CEO of this company. You cannot write emails like that without proofreading them."

I said, "Honey, I proofread that email twice!" So, while I still needed to do some serious work on my writing skills, I was at least comforted by the fact that our people were committing to our company in such inspiring ways.

As our culture, onboarding, and sense of purpose began to align, we were also able to take wider steps in pursuit of our company goals. You can do that when you have the right people in the right seats. If the ship is in full working order, I learned, making decisions regarding rougher seas or taking riskier routes is a little less worrisome for a leader. For us, that meant sailing into the deep, dreadful waters of policy changes.

Ask any number of business leaders about policy, and most will tell you it's one of the cornerstones of successful business management. As such, to remove or drastically alter your policies could have disastrous outcomes. In our industry especially, everyone seemed to think the best policy led to the best results. At the time, my HR team thought so, too, but I didn't agree. I thought that too much policy was time consuming, and was ultimately responsible for holding people back from doing their best work. After all, if you have the best people in the best place for them, why not let them do what it is they do best? Beyond that, an abundance of policies usually leads to employees either not following them or working harder to follow them and then resenting their company later. With no mid-level operations management to enforce the policies we did have, I knew we could no longer rely on policies to oversee the actions of our staff.

We were willing to admit that we didn't know everything about everything, but we were also willing to do the necessary work so we could bet that our people did. Once we got to this point, policy carried much less weight in everyone's mind. We decided that instead of a list of policies our staff would have to memorize and obey, we would give them a simple decision-making process they could follow. We told our people, "Before you do something, just ask yourself three questions: Is it the right thing to do for the customer? Is it the right thing to do for our company, based on our purpose and values? And finally, is it something you're willing to be accountable for?" If the answer was yes, yes, and yes, don't ask for permission—just do it.

At the time, our primary target was to empower people working on the frontlines in hopes that it would increase morale and in turn, provide value to our customers, with the ultimate goal being one step closer in turning employees within our ranks into stakeholders in our business. I was told this was nearly impossible—you couldn't have a stakeholder who wasn't a shareholder. We wanted to build on our initiative to help every employee take pride in their work, and to feel that they and their job were integral to their employer's success.

My HR manager thought I was nuts, arguing that without any policy the company would descend into chaos and we would never scale the business.

We were at a fork in the road. I wanted to continue with the decision-making process and roll it out company wide. My HR manager wanted to update and execute company policy nationwide. To me, this was a complete conflict. On one hand, we were telling people, "Take your brain back and follow a simple decision-making process, but … before you do, make sure to check your policy book to see if it's in the rules." I did what any unorthodox leader would do—I called the management team into the boardroom and asked them to vote on it. We were either going to update our policy book or throw it out completely and stick to our simplified decision-making process. We found ourselves in a deadlock at four for and four against. I decided it was time to bring in the perspective of our frontline staff. As stakeholders in our company, I had to give them a voice.

So, I called Sue Mousseau, a superstar security officer, who worked at an Ontario hospital. We had never met, but Sue knew who I was. I said, "Hi, Sue, how are you? I am about to make a really big decision about the company and I am hoping to get your opinion. What do you think about us throwing out the policy book and replacing it completely with the individual decision-making process?" You could hear a pin drop on the phone call during a very long moment of silence. Security guards are never asked such big questions about the direction of their company.

After a long pause she said, "I think we should get rid of policy. I love the decision-making process, and policy does not allow people to think for themselves."

She was right. Policies are like rules, and rules are made for children. How would I grow a business and turn employees into stakeholders with a bunch of people around me that I treated like children? It was time we gave everyone their brains back and let them make decisions for themselves. And I know that during that phone call, Sue Mousseau was converted into a passionate stakeholder. She would never leave our company, because she now had a big voice at the table for one of the biggest business decisions to date.

The next day, we rolled out the decision-making process, and threw out the policy book once and for all. Needless to say, the HR manager and I parted ways. Everyone had told us it couldn't be done, that too much freedom would lead to one type of doom or another, driven by misconduct and chaos. But I knew our people better than anyone else did. I watched with my own two eyes as our people stepped up to the plate, without being asked, to help our company push its limits, and I was so excited about it I was actually losing sleep. We had stepped up to the challenge for one simple but imperative reason: our purpose! To win, a revolutionary spirit and its ensuing ideas had to succeed. But like any major change in how a company operates, we had to be all in. The changes needed to be swift. Hesitating to follow through or leaving pieces of the old hanging will only create pain points attributed to confusion and dysfunction. People were immediately converted to stakeholders by allowing them to finally make decisions. This huge change pushed our culture to new heights, and our clients took notice, too. Things were finally getting done at the site level in the most efficient way.

Today, companies use onboarding to train new hires based on their job description, which essentially says, "Here are the ten things you're going to do for your job." A job description doesn't tell you what the outcomes have to be—it doesn't say, "Here's what a home run looks like in all of these job tasks, and here's how we're going to hold you accountable." So, we added what we called "descriptive role outcomes" which explained the outcomes of a rock star in their respective position. Then we explained how outcomes' performance quality was measured. That allowed us to be clearer with team members about our expectations. That was one step in the right direction to keep us ahead of our competition. But the question we still needed to address was, even though people knew how to hit home runs in all of these different tasks, would they really enjoy them?

I found my answer in a team member named Carolyn Dawson. Carolyn was working in our financial department, where she had been rated as an A-player in her position. I heard through the grapevine that she was looking for a job because she was unhappy. The notion that a team member was unhappy, no matter where they were in the company, always bothered me more than anything else. We had worked hard to build this great culture, and someone's unhappy? That was always a button for me. Maybe it was an ego thing, but I was so proud that I couldn't understand how someone else could not be happy.

I decided to take Carolyn out for lunch and get to the bottom of her unhappiness.

"So, Carolyn," I got right to the point, "I hear you're not happy here."

She said, "Well, I love the company, but I don't really like what I'm doing."

At the time, she was reporting to our finance controller, so I asked, "Okay, well, what's your dream job? What would you love to do?"

She said, "I always wanted to work with the police force, and I wanted to implement training and policy for police officers."

At that point, it was clear to me. "We don't have any policy, as you know, so you can't execute policy here. Instead of policy, though, if you really think about it, we have a ton of systems and processes. So, what if you could help coach those systems and processes rather than policies?" Carolyn loved the idea, and a new position was born.

Carolyn brought to light some other gaps in our company as well. I wanted to know why we had talented and dedicated people doing jobs they didn't want to do. Statistically, people enjoy maybe 60 percent of what they do in their jobs, and that's a liberal estimate. We decided to organize what I referred to as a "task mapping system." We started the process with management, and I had every department participate—HR, finance, and sales (there was no operations department at the time). I said, "Everyone write down each task you're responsible for in your department. Then, I want you to get organized according to who is primarily responsible for which task. Then, go down the list and highlight the task in red or green; green representing what you love, and red representing what you don't enjoy."

The results were interesting. The list read like a total mismatch. We had people undertaking a number of items they really didn't like simply because they loved the company. To me, that is a death by a thousand cuts, so I told everyone in company-wide communications, "Look, we're going to reengineer our functions. I want everyone to be accountable for job tasks that they truly enjoy doing on a day-to-day basis." Furthermore, I asked them to list their name next to items they would like to learn about: "If you think there's something interesting, put your name there." These were day-to-day tasks, not necessarily projects, so it was very easy to say, "If you don't like doing something, sign up to learn another task." Of course, everyone was given a short period of time to hit home runs consistently, or we would have to move them.

This process really opened my eyes. Even if we were finally culturally aligned, are staff's passions and skills were still misaligned with things the company needed done. Through this process, Task Mapping™ was born.

Once we had success throwing out all the job descriptions for managers, we still had gaps; there were still leftover tasks people were stuck with that no one within the management team was excited to take on. So we decided to push our task mapping process down to the frontline staff, including full-time/part-time guards, security supervisors and coordinators. We began to see even more traction from the frontline employees as they became laser focused on single tasks that we could never seem to get done. It was interesting when we found people who aligned well with a new function.

Not only could we reorganize job positions so that people did what they actually enjoyed doing more often, but the mapping process did two other important things for us:

First, it showed us where our gaps were, quickly and easily, as they were self-reported in real time. Second, it allowed the company to start managing by process, not by title or org chart. Our people owned the process—they were essentially the CEO of a specific company task. In some cases, a frontline staff member even held me accountable for a company process being completed. I loved it. As you can imagine, I absolutely couldn't have accomplished this without my ego being put in check and putting full faith in the process of turning into a results-driven organization.

If, for example, we looked at the names in red and saw that no one liked doing a specific function, we would look for someone within the company who would like to do that. We would pay them by outcome instead of hourly. If we couldn't find anyone internally who wanted to perform a specific function, we went to a third-party contractor. It took some time and plenty of patience, but in the end, after cleaning out the junk resulting from mismatched functions, we were humming like a well-oiled machine and we had an army of people to lean on!

Realistically, when you give someone a job description, as discussed, they will be passionate about some of the things on the list, if you're lucky. That means when they get up in the morning, they're only happy about doing half of their job. The other half? Not so much. Think about it—do you really think people like all the tasks in their job descriptions? Don't kid yourself. There isn't a lot an employer can do about that. No job is pleasant and fun all the time. It is, after all, a job. But if people love only 50 percent of their job's functions, they aren't going to hit a home run 100 percent of the time. Like so many companies, we missed that. It didn't matter that we said, "Here's what a grand slam looks like. Here's how we measure it," when employees were thinking, "I don't swing that kind of bat. I don't really know how to play that type of game. Hell, I don't even like that type of game."

Understandably, no one kicks up a fuss when you hire them. They just say, "Great, I got a job. This seems like a good company, and I like the majority of my job functions." But in their gut, they know they are going to drop the ball on nearly half of their functions. Task mapping ties specific job functions to specific people based on their likes and dislikes. We used the map to guide our onboarding process as well, using it to tell us who was going to do what function based on what they really liked to do. The results were incredible. We had smoother workforce alignment, improved work quality, reduced training costs, and a lower turnover rate after implementing the system. In turn, real work-life balance became attainable for our staff.

Even though the system was working well, there were still some projects left over that people were accountable for, but weren't excited about doing. One of these items was our company newsletter. For years, the company newsletter had been a pain in my side. I had passed it off at least a dozen times to different people on our team, only to have it fall back in my lap months later. But the real issue wasn't the newsletter itself. The real issue was the process around why the newsletter hadn't yet found its forever home.

We started a process called insourcing. We had access to roughly fifteen hundred employees who, although they had signed up to be security guards, probably also had other passions and skills, like the rest of us. We needed to tap into those skills and utilize our people's passions beyond security services. We put the company newsletter out for auction. We talked to anybody and everybody to see if they would be interested, and sure enough, a security guard in our own backyard named Stephanie Cooper, who worked primarily at a local university, said she would be more than happy to take over that project. We negotiated to pay Stephanie an additional $50 when the newsletter was finished each month. Not only was the newsletter finally sent out on time, but it had more valuable information for staff than I had ever seen before, simply because someone was passionate about the task. With results like this, it was time to push it even further.

Around the same time, we were thinking about bringing on an occupational health and safety manager, which would cost $50,000 – $60,000 per year. No one in our HR department had an OHS specialty. Again, we decided to push this out to the guards in the field, our extended Source family, and see if anyone might have a background in this area. We broke down all the specific OHS functions we needed to, like site safety and audits.

Sure enough, one of our guards—Paul Crawford, again—shot his hand up and said he was an occupational health and safety expert. Not only did Paul take on the challenge to be our national occupational health and safety officer, he also recruited five other security officers across the country with similar backgrounds to assist him in taking on the project. We went from having no potential candidates to six at a cost of $0. All six were so thrilled to be involved in something outside of their mundane security tasks that they wouldn't accept any compensation for this work. Paul took the lead and organized monthly calls and put time aside to review all documents relative to OHS. Although he wouldn't accept a dime for this additional work, we of course wanted to show him how much we valued his initiative. We built in a raise to his hourly billable wage, along with a cell phone allowance, costing two thousand dollars per year—now that's value!

If you're thinking that most of these stories and process successes don't pertain to your industry, you couldn't be more wrong—I strongly advise you to put this book down and go ask your best friend to delicately wedgie you to bring you back to reality.

> IF YOU'RE THINKING THAT MOST OF THESE STORIES AND PROCESS SUCCESSES DON'T PERTAIN TO YOUR INDUSTRY, YOU COULDN'T BE MORE WRONG.

Every business needs their books reconciled, and nobody likes to do it. Reconciliation was the next project for our insourcing model.

After putting this out to our extended family once again, we found a guard who worked the back shift at a trucking yard in Vancouver who had more accounting accolades than most of our accounting department combined. We paid him $100 per month to reconcile the bank, and the outcome was beyond what we could have hoped for. In our company, bank reconciliation was always behind, sometimes by four to five months. This individual was so focused, it was typically done at the end of each week.

Since things were going so well, I thought, "why not keep that momentum going?" I had a few projects in mind for a while. So often, as entrepreneurs, we come up with (what we think is) a brilliant idea in the middle of the night, we rush to the office the next morning begging people to implement them, but people just look at us like we are crazy! There are clear differences between regular company tasks and new company initiatives, however, these projects could still add a lot of value to the company. I ended up pushing a lot of these projects out to various staff, who were happy to accept the challenge.

Next came the internal website we used to source products to ensure that our guards had proper equipment. One of our guards in Vancouver, who loved IT and e-commerce, asked to take this on. It was a project that sat idle for almost two years, and he had the site up and running with items ready to sell and ship directly to our staff within forty-eight hours.

These projects were funneled out as quickly as they came in. We had designed a true community of people within the Source family who loved to do the things they loved to do. If the outcomes around day-to-day tasks weren't enough to excite you, the next phase organically fell into my lap moved from tactical to strategic thinking among our converted stakeholders.

One day I received a call from Ashwani, who had earlier purchased our company truck, asking if I could carve out some time to meet with him on my next trip to Toronto. On my arrival, I decided to bring him into a meeting at Toronto City Airport. He was so proud to come to this meeting, as frontline staff are never involved in prospective client meetings. In fact, as this was a site meeting for an RFP (Request for Proposal) there were roughly fifteen other companies at this initial meeting for a walkthrough at the airport. When Ashwani showed up, he spotted two of his old senior managers from G4s, gave them a little smile and a wink, and watched their surprise as he strolled past them with me. I was just as proud.

After an incredibly boring walkthrough. Ashwani and I went to a local coffee shop. He turned to me with a serious face and said, "I have something I need to show you."

He opened his laptop and I was shocked by what he showed me. He presented a fifteen-slide PowerPoint about how Source Security could expand into his native country of India. He had everything properly mapped out, from the cities we would enter first to which clients we would target, along with resources and support to help us get off the ground.

I was blown away. Think about it for a second. This guy had worked in the security industry for fifteen years. He hated every other company he had previously worked for, and although he was doing the exact same day-to-day job, at the same site, something was now different for him. It was not a fancy title or a quarterly bonus that shifted him to a stakeholder; it was that he had the power to make decisions in an environment where his vision was welcomed.

Getting my company to the point where frontline staff were thinking strategically about my business was unfathomable, and yet we had done it. It had always been terribly challenging to get senior managers to do this in the past. They were too busy running around putting out fires and, in some cases, trying to look authoritative and barking out orders.

We were quickly discovering the amount of untapped brain-power within our company was endless. I was embarrassed I had missed this for more than a decade.

SOLVING THE ENGAGEMENT PUZZLE

In today's workplace, no matter the industry, engagement is driving a new vision for the old rules. Companies are learning that in order to track, engage, and retain top talent, they have to change the way they think about rules and the employees who must adhere to them. We were fortunate enough to start evolving our engagement strategy before it was necessary in our industry, but no matter when you do it, it's important that you begin the process by listening to your workers. Our growth was directly related to collective input.

The more we learned about engagement at Source, the more obvious the correlation between our culture and productivity became. What I discovered early on was that to really engage the workforce, I had to step up as a leader on a regular basis to explain what was happening in the workplace and why. Employees need to feel like they're a part of their company's progress. They need to understand why a particular change is going to be good for them and their department so the inevitable pain of change is more bearable. Your people also need to buy into the ideas. They are driving the change, after all, so they need to believe in the direction they're being asked to go if your company is to have any hope of getting there.

Otherwise, their sense of purpose will grow murky, their sense of job stability will wane, and their morale and productivity will eventually plummet. There is no way around it: you must talk—and more importantly, listen—to the people who are involved in any shift of a company's direction.

For any leader to engage their workers, they first have to know who their workers are. That calls for company leaders to learn a number of things about their employees, from their strengths and weaknesses to their constraints and what is needed to help resolve them. These are all variables that, frankly, companies did not have to care very much about when workers were regarded as a disposable feature in the corporate business model.

Understanding the individual employee and customizing work styles is certainly a more empathetic form of leadership, but it didn't come at the expense of profit for Source. Quite the opposite, in fact, as our focus was squarely on results. And the results were undeniably good, from workplace culture and workforce morale to the bottom line.

But of course, in line with the old saying "You don't know what you don't know," we ran into a snag. We had a very challenging client in Dartmouth, Nova Scotia, in the auto shipping and receiving industry. This particular site had horrible morale and was considered a very chaotic environment, so it was difficult for us to operate in. Our client had gone through several of our site managers and coordinators but eventually landed on an individual who had a ton of ex-military experience, named John Burke. We thought we had our winner.

As it turned out, we were dead wrong. As you can imagine, military-trained individuals are used to very strict policies and procedures, not to mention a serious chain of command. We no longer operated under a chain of command, and our policies and procedures had dissipated, so John really struggled in that environment. Furthermore, John was someone we had brought on before we started our empathy screening—he wouldn't have passed. I decided to go down and meet with him to see if I could help.

On my arrival, John gave me a laundry list of issues he was having with the staff, the site, and even the client. In that business, we had to keep things simple, so I asked him, "If I were to show up for my shift and you had ten minutes to explain five key things I needed to do for the client to feel like we hit a home run in providing good service, what would those five things be?"

John was taken aback by this. He said, "Ron, I'm not quite sure you read my resume before coming out here, but I have multiple years of military experience: thirty-plus, to be exact."

Of course, the aggressive Aries came out and I quickly retaliated: "I don't care if you were the head of the FBI for a hundred years. I'm asking you a simple question so we can work together to get this site smoothed out and operating under the new Source standard."

John crossed his arms, became standoffish, and again began explaining his extensive experience in the military.

I believe he felt his years of military experience gave him authority above these simple questions and methods of working. At this point, I had had enough. I said to him, "Look, pal, we're both grown adults here and it's obvious that culturally this company is not a good fit for you."

"You're *firing* me?" He asked, completely perplexed.

"No," I replied, "I think we both just need to come to the consensus that although your experience is highly valued and will be put to excellent use at another security company, I think we can both agree Source is not the right fit for you."

John abruptly grabbed his belongings and walked out the door.

This site was a disaster, but at that moment it hit me: "Holy shit, this is now my responsibility, and I have no idea who is supposed to be managing which post at what time, or how they are supposed to do it." Nobody in HR, sales, or finance had these answers, either. It was really up to me to untangle this mess. It was definitely a taste of humble pie—I felt like I was back in the early days of Source, spending my evenings at home scheduling security guards on my kitchen floor.

Did I mention this happened a week before Christmas, inarguably the most difficult time to find staff to work? Here I was on Christmas Eve making phone calls to fill shifts for security guards. I was determined not to let this get in the way of all of the progress we had made to date.

At the time, a few on our leadership team wanted to play the "I told you so" game, making note that we didn't have any mid-level managers, so I had to do the work myself. But I wasn't willing to retreat from this new model of pushing all managerial duties to ground level, not until we had exhausted every resource.

I was convinced that if we had the right coordinator in place, it would essentially fix our problem. I had my eye on a gentleman named Gary Graham, so I approached him to see if he was up for the challenge. Sure enough, he was our guy. Gary was interested in using his prior skills in leadership and organization to find creative ways to untangle the mess at this site. He had never been given the opportunity to actually use his brain at a security site, and he completely turned the site around within a few weeks. The client was thrilled.

Needless to say, we still had a major continuity gap, and someone needed to step into the role. We needed to ensure this situation didn't happen again, and put a few things into motion. It was evident we were missing a sense of community within our organization. This was something I knew needed to be tackled if the model was to suffice. All the site supervisors were then divided into their own teams. Those teams had weekly phone calls during which they would talk about the highs and lows (challenges) of their site. So, if someone's low was that a person kept showing up late, the group would, one-by-one, share their experience on how they fixed the same issue in the past. We were putting them into their own micro-forums, creating a community of resources, training, coaching and support. We also ensured they were all cross trained at each other's sites.

They began leaning on each other to help solve problems. I had been on many of these weekly phone calls and couldn't believe what I was hearing. I was tickled by the problem-solving. When our people in these mini-communities asked for help, everyone jumped in. It was really magical and inspiring for us to see the amount of work that could be accomplished when people had a sense of autonomy and purpose, and now, a sense of community too. We never could have achieved this level of community and support with mid-level managers.

Finally, we made sure the site supervisor (the second in command) at every site had the exact same training as the site coordinator. This ensured that if something were to happen to the coordinator, the supervisor could easily jump in as the acting manager. We were finally operating efficiently at the site level, and it became clear to everyone that we actually did not need midlevel management. In fact, our efficiencies going forward increased even further.

At its center, everything we were doing was based on the premise that employees will do their very best work once you've helped them find what they love most about their job. Sometimes that means leading them by the hand, and sometimes that just means getting out of their way. In any case, you can't know how to get the best out of a person if you do not first know who they are. And when you toss out the rule book, you're putting a hell of a lot more trust in your people to govern themselves. The more they respect themselves, their job, and their teammates, the more efficiently things will run. Of course, if your employees are going to function as a team with movable positions and accountable tasks, they're going to need more than a boss. They're going to need a coach.

LIFE AFTER TAKEOFF

CHAPTER 8

BE A COACH, NOT A BOSS

As you may have guessed, I have always been unorthodox in how I do business. Like all other business leaders, however, I had to deal with the tough reality of being the decision maker for others. Among the most difficult tasks a leader has to undertake is letting people go. It is an inevitable part of the job, and over my fifteen years of running a business, I had to do it more times than I'd like to count. It is hard and painful, even if the employee in question deserves to be fired.

To reduce the number of people we let go, I had always tried to coach people rather than control them. I really wanted our company to run like a sports team. I didn't wait for someone's quarterly review or yearly review to critique their performance. I did it in real time. If someone had a great play, so to speak, I made sure to tell them after. If they didn't play well, if they fell on their face or made a mistake, I made sure to ask the right questions and allow them the space to answer them (sometimes with exceptionally long pauses). As a coach, the day you have all of the answers is the day you might miss the most obvious play that may just solidify your win. The skills that you applied to your company to get to the first million are the same skills that will inevitably get in your way as you attempt to grow to $10 million—unless you have made the transition from being the one and only problem solver to being a fantastic coach of a whole team of problem solvers.

It felt more natural to me, and I have always tried to let my instincts guide how I do things in business. Unfortunately, that wasn't a leadership style that was wildly popular among some of my previous management staff, who valued a more conventionally structured management process with paperwork and reviews—everything I found boring, insincere, and ultimately ineffective—and so I had to let many of them go in order to secure leadership alignment at all levels.

I never documented anything, either. The reason I didn't do that in my entire career of owning businesses was that my job as president—and, I believe, our jobs as leaders—was to build relationships. We are supposed to connect with people, allow them to be vulnerable, and make sure they have everything they need to be successful. People can't put their best foot forward if they're walking on eggshells.

Bringing in paperwork to "write up" employees for small infractions while threatening them with suspension or termination creates dissonance. All of a sudden, you're looking at me like I'm the enemy instead of your leader. We are not working with each other, which was probably the cause of the problem in the first place. Now you might be saying to yourself, "Wow, I don't trust Ron anymore. He's building a case on me."

Even though labor standards say you should always document infractions and staff conflicts, when I looked at companies that had documented those things, I noticed they had been taken to the Labor Board more than anyone else. In the fifteen years I was at Source, no direct report had gone to a lawyer or to the Labor Board on me.

I'm confident this was the case because I always treated people like humans. If the job wasn't right for them, I got them to understand that it wasn't and that it was time to move on. Once they understood why, I would help them move on. That was part of my process, but it was by no means perfect.

As we were growing, my HR department really challenged me about this approach and said, "Look, Ron, we have to document something."

If you recall earlier in the story, our previous HR manager, Jodi, who at one point left the company and then returned, was now a stakeholder who had found her voice. She challenged me by saying, "We need to have some kind of balance. We can't scale this process. You have a unique skill, but we need a system around it." She was right.

So, I called a meeting with all of our team and said, "Your job is to coach the people you work with, to coach the guards out in the field on whatever your skill is. You're not their manager. You're there to support them and coach them." I wanted to get people to shift the way they thought about working with each other, so we reversed our organizational chart. Our front-line staff were now at the top of the org chart. As the CEO, I was now at the bottom, meaning I was there to support everyone else in the field. Managers, HR personnel, finance roles—everyone was now responsible for helping the frontline employees succeed. I officially changed my title and became the CSO, or Chief Support Officer.

Nearly all companies out there use disciplinary forms, but we threw that out and invented a "coaching sheet." A coaching sheet is the same concept as a disciplinary form, just flipped on its head. Whereas a disciplinary form might tell a worker what they did wrong and what their punishment would be, our coaching sheet provided a more thorough support for working through the problem.

That conversation went something like this: "You're struggling with X. Let's talk about it. Let's talk about consequences around the situation. Does our company have an internal system or process that will alleviate this problem? If so, have you been clearly trained on it? If not, let's you and I build one. What support do you need from me going forward?" The most critical part of this process was asking team members how we could support them to do a better job, not telling them what needed to be done. After quick deliberation around the issue, we would always ensure that our company purpose, values, and decision-making process were aligned with the strategy we agreed on. The employee, and the manager, would then sign off to hold the manager accountable to the coaching process. That flipped the entire dynamic from "boss" and "worker" to teammates. Through the coaching process, we were putting people's destinies in their own hands by telling them that if they chose to behave in ways that did not align with our values or purpose, they would be choosing to leave the company. We made that very clear, and it kept us out of a lot of trouble.

For our industry in particular, this was an extremely unusual management style. Among the industry's frontline employees, there was little to no trust in leadership. They felt there was no support—or as one individual told me, like they were "lint on the floor." So, this change told people at every level that they mattered to the organization. The goal was to get workers to say, "Wow, if I am valued by the organization, then maybe I should put more into my work." That mindset really lifted the morale, productivity, and accountability within the entire company.

If you think of it again in terms of a sports team, the intentions are clearer. Most companies employ a tactic where they ask employees what they are going to do to fix a problem, or a "ninety-day plan" to improve their performance. Imagine coming off the basketball court and your coach saying to you, "Look, you're struggling with three-pointer shots. You tell me what you're going to do in the next ninety days to shoot better threes." That never happens in sports, because it would be terrible coaching. Instead, the coach says, "I was watching your three-point shot, and we can make it better. You need to tuck your elbow in, I'm also going to get you an expert on three-pointers to help you with that." That's what we did. We gave people a friend within the company rather than a disciplinarian, and the results were tremendous.

I ONLY WANT YOUR BEST

In the early days at Source, I spent a lot of time checking people's work. I might ask a salesperson to build a proposal, only to have to tear it apart and do it myself. I knew that either people were not giving me their best, or they were but their best wasn't even close to what our standards should have been. It was one or the other, and I needed to cut through all the BS to find the answer to that question.

I sat everyone in the company down and said, "Guys, we have a new standard. From now on, I only want your best. Everything you do has to be your absolute, 110 percent best." I'd go to each person and ask, "Can you commit to your best?" Then I explained to them that I would analyze every project they brought to me, looking for the highest standard. "If you can commit to giving me 110 percent on everything I'm going to look at and everything you do here, then you have to understand one thing: if you bring me your best and it is garbage, this may not be the place for you to work, and it's going to give us the answer pretty quickly."

That approach did two things for us. For people who really could produce great work, their work went up. They brought their best every time, even if they sometimes had to go back and try again. I'd say, "Look, before I open this, is this your best work?"

They might say, "You know what? It is not."

I'd say, "I'm going to do us both a favor, then. Take it away and bring it back when it's your absolute best and you think you can't do any better. That's what I'm looking for."

Other times, people had said, "Yes, Ron, it's my best." And we would both know the work was crap and it was time for that person to leave. This was a black-and-white coaching mechanism that gave me a lot of clarity around a person's commitment and performance. Plus, it saved me a lot of time, because our folks who were not really giving it their all now had a new standard to live up to. Those who didn't want to put in the extra effort to reach it, left. That was fine with me, because it told me their heart wasn't in the game. These were good people. If it were a different company, a different industry, a different position, or even a different time in their lives, things might have been different. In those cases, I told them their best should be somewhere else. "It is not here," I said. "Let's find you a place where you can be your best." The truth came out through the work. You can't hide when you're asked for your best.

COACHING CULTURAL ALIGNMENT

Our culture was continuing to move in the right direction, and the question I kept getting from other business leaders was: "Aside from reducing turnover, what is the real ROI with culture in your company?"

Obviously, that's often an intangible assessment. But other times it comes up when you're in a jam. As an example, several years ago, we lost a major client that provided 20 percent of our overall revenue. They were a big real estate management company we had been servicing for three years when their contract went up for bid. We didn't win the contract, because we were overconfident in our relationship and raised our price, which they rejected. We missed it completely. The question should have been, "What would we price this project if we didn't have it?" That was a big shift in our business on the bidding process afterward, but because we didn't employ that strategy until it was too late, we had to come up with a way to recoup 20 percent of our revenue in a hurry. We were losing $30,000 a month because we had overheads in place, and the bleed was going to kill us.

At the time, I had about fifteen people in management positions from sales operations, HR, and finance. I was vulnerable with them and said, "OK, here's the reality of the situation. We lost the contract. We all know that. We're bleeding now. So, I'm going to put some options in front of you. Are you all open to taking a pay cut for six months? That can be in two different forms. It can be a straight pay cut, or you can work four days a week. I'll allow both. The reality is, if we do this together, then everybody stays. If we don't, I have to let one or two people go. Even you, who I'm speaking to right now, could be on that list. I just want to make that clear. Everyone is at risk here."

The response was unexpected. Everyone, even people who had only worked with the company for three to six months, said, "I'm in. I'll take the pay cut." No one took the four days a week. Everyone said, "I'll work through and I'll take the pay cut." I took a 20 percent pay cut for six months, while the rest took a 10 percent cut for six months. I couldn't have pulled that off in the earlier years at Source, before we had cultural alignment. It's simply abnormal for people to band together to that extent in the workplace, especially given the uniqueness of our structure. We were spread out across the country, so there was very little personal relationship between these people besides meeting at our quarterly planning sessions. And yet, they were all willing to fight for the rest of the team. I was very impressed, and for the first time I thought, "You know what, this culture thing is paying off in spades." Not to mention other impacts, such as the fact our Labor Board threats were down to virtually none, our workplace claims had been drastically reduced, overtime was way down, and customer service satisfaction through net promoter scores was at an all-time high.

To return to the sports team analogy once again, if you're part of a team, you want what's best for the team. If that means you have to sit on the bench, you'll do it. If it means going out and sacrificing yourself for the benefit of the team, you'll do that, too. For the first time, the solidarity within our group was on full display and I couldn't have been happier—or more relieved.

> TO RETURN TO THE SPORTS TEAM ANALOGY ONCE AGAIN, IF YOU'RE PART OF A TEAM, YOU WANT WHAT'S BEST FOR THE TEAM.

What I learned most by transitioning from a boss to a coach mentality had to do with balance. When a company knows its purpose, has defined its values and culture, and has successfully established its brand and operational structure, keeping it all running smoothly depends on how well each element stays aligned with the other. By working to align your goals with the goals of others, combining your strengths to reach them together, everyone wins. And if you are grateful, you will gain something from everyone. Everyone is a teacher, but it is up to you as a coach to discover what you might learn from them.

CHAPTER 9

COLLABORATE OR PERISH

Y ou may not always need a doctor to give you a proper diagnosis. Don't believe me? I'll prove it. A few years ago, I launched a company called CelebConnect, which I recently sold. In short, we matched clients in need of a speaker, emcee, music artist, or comedian with corporation conferences and brands. Around the time we launched, we asked author of the Canadian best seller: *Wealthy Barber*, and former *Dragon's Den* star, David Chilton, to come speak in front of a group in Halifax.

David liked our model and wanted to help us out, so he and I exchanged a dozen or so emails and a few phone calls to work out the specifics. Fast-forward to the day of the event, and as he was getting ready to go on, David looked at me and said, "Hey, Ron, I have a question for you."

I said, "Yeah, what's that?"

"Are you dyslexic?" he asked.

I was taken by complete surprise. "Um, no. Well, I don't know. I don't think so. I doubt it."

"Are you sure?" he pressed.

"Why do you ask?" I said, growing more curious.

"Now that we have been going back and forth, I have read some of your emails and I think you might be dyslexic."

I started laughing, but after I thought about it for a few minutes, I thought he could be right. I went out and took three online dyslexic tests, and I likely scored the highest I have ever scored on any test in my life. Later, I went to an expert to confirm the diagnosis. Everything finally made sense regarding my struggles with reading and writing. And the irony was that I was basically diagnosed by David Chilton at the age of thirty-seven, which was hilarious and informative at the same time.

I knew I had ADHD my whole life, and it was confirmed later on as an adult. I had started meditating for that, but dyslexia was a different story. I had been trying to find coping mechanisms or tools I could use to help my situation, but you can't solve a problem without knowing what the problem is to begin with. Now I tell people up front that I am dyslexic, and warn them that they probably will not be able to read any of my writing. It is akin to a different language, one that sometimes requires others to translate.

My dyslexia was one reason why collaboration was so important to me, and my ADHD was perhaps the source of my respect for curiosity. Combined, what could have been challenges that set me back actually became the driving force for one of our core values: continuous improvement. I grill applicants and employees about their level of curiosity. If they were not curious—if they didn't want to learn, collaborate with others, and grow—then I knew they didn't have a place in our company. Curiosity, to me, was a characteristic trait that people either had or didn't have. It was also an attribute that would allow them to be successful and live our core values.

Vetting people based on curiosity and collaborative input allowed us to streamline the business by cutting out dead weight before it began to weigh us down. We knew that if we had a good system in place for onboarding the right people, we could hire people who would do their jobs so well they could manage themselves. Doing so also allowed us to cut out much of our midlevel management, of course, but it did much more than that if you count the small ways in which having great people made us more versatile.

We used to track sick days and vacation days, for example. That created mounds and mounds of HR work, and so much of it was a complete waste of time and resources. I began research on the issue and thought, "We have a different culture now. Why can't we do things differently?"

With our new model of Task Mapping™, and focusing on results, we no longer had one person trying to do a hundred things. We had twenty people supporting each other to get things done at a micro level. This took a tremendous amount off of our day-to-day plate. That, coupled with our focus on outcomes as opposed to time sheets, gave our people a much better work-life balance.

We were about to conduct our year end planning at the time this was going on, and I asked a group of entrepreneurs, "What kind of vacation should I give?" Everyone felt we should follow labour standards. I had just read a book by Cameron Herold, former COO of 1-800-Got-Junk, called *Double Double*. Cameron proposed that everyone should have five weeks of vacation from the time they start. I thought long and hard about that, because I was going to take a big risk, but I believed we had the capacity and the right culture to pull it off.

Standing before an EO (Entrepreneurs Organization) forum, I said, "I'm thinking it is either five weeks, or unlimited vacation." I then ran the idea past my close friend and neighbor, Alex Halef, who told me the idea was nuts.

"Ron, if you give unlimited vacation, it will never work. You're out of your mind."

It wasn't exactly the vote of confidence I was hoping for, so I asked for a second opinion. One after another, entrepreneurs and business leaders challenged me on the idea. They said, "Maybe five weeks, but unlimited is insane."

I tossed and turned, thinking about the issue. I was facilitating our quarterly planning session that would convene in the coming weeks. I planned to make an announcement about vacation and sick leave, but now I was a little anxious about what I was going to do.

I often go for a bike ride to clear my head, and doing so one afternoon, the answer dawned on me. If we did five weeks, we would still have to track it. I didn't want to do that, and I was certain there was no one in the company who enjoyed tracking people's vacation, so it was one of the tasks left off the HR task mapping list. That was one piece of the answer. The other was my belief that if someone got five weeks of vacation, they would certainly take five weeks of vacation. I believed at the time that if vacation time were unlimited, everything would be based on outcomes and outputs even more. If you are hitting home runs, meeting or exceeding the company's expectations around results, why would it matter where you do it from or when you do it? If people didn't have to come to the office anymore and had unlimited vacation, I thought they would probably only take three weeks of vacation, because they would be less burnt out and sick of being at work.

I decided to test my theory and announced, to much surprise and excitement, what every employee wants to hear: unlimited vacation.

"We'll never track another day," I said. "You can work from wherever you want. I also decided to shut my own personal office down—I'm done with my office. I don't need to have one anymore." I wasn't joking, either. I put a sofa in my old office and said anybody could use it. I also removed my parking space and just parked wherever I could when I came to the building.

Some of my staff were bewildered, maybe even a little wary of the notion they could go on vacation for however long they wanted. Jim Kennedy, a top sales rep, challenged me first. He stood up and said, "Let me ask you a question. If my targets for the quarter are $1 million and I hit that in the first month of the quarter, you're telling me I can take two months off?"

I said, "Absolutely. If you hit your targets in the first month, take the rest of the quarter off. We may change your targets for the next quarter because you're doing so well, though, but for this quarter, absolutely, if you hit your targets take two months off, I have no problem with that. Take your family and do whatever you want for the rest of the quarter."

Jim smiled wide and said, "Okay. Sounds good." It may surprise you, but after we launched our unlimited vacation initiative, no one ever took advantage of it in the three years I remained with Source. People came and went as they pleased. If they needed to go to the doctor, they went to the doctor. We didn't track it. If they were sick, they were sick. If they wanted to go on vacation, they went. At the same time, they still had a job to do. If they were responsible for an important duty, they had the autonomy to find someone to do that task correctly if they were going to be unplugged. That was the way we went, and it worked out incredibly well. We were now 100 percent results driven. We needed a strong team culture and reliable employees to make it work, but I can assure you I will never own a company again that will not have unlimited vacation. It worked that well. But looking back, I know if I had announced that a few years prior, before I had the right culture, my neighbor Alex would have been right and it would not have gone well at all. Having unlimited vacation became a huge conversation piece with clients and a major recruiting tool as well.

I was able to make such a radical change because we had essentially deconstructed the entire management model from the top down. All of our operational functions down to the ground level were split among many people rather than one or two, allowing everyone to take on more of a supportive role within the management structure. For instance, an operations manager who used to look after twenty-five supervisors now had their job functions divided among those twenty-five supervisors. Essentially our staff members now had direct access to the clients, to the entire staff, and to our resources and relationships at the head office level. We were also able to pay front line coordinators, supervisors and staff a little more because we gutted the operations and regional manager positions and our COO position, as well as their offices.

I will say that nearly everyone fought me on these changes, especially tenured management who had been around for years. No one in the industry had ever trusted the frontline people, and my own people told me, "You can't do this. It is not going to work, because it is not sustainable." Not only was it sustainable and easier to scale, but it was also more profitable and made us much nimbler, not to mention our people were happier. Our clients also loved the new model, as they could now deal with people directly at the site instead of calling a mid-level manager or senior manager at an office. They now had a decision maker right in front of them.

As you try to implement change in a system like the one we created, the process can be more difficult and time consuming on the front end. If I wanted to change the way something was done even on the front line, I couldn't send a memo across the country and say, "Hey, everybody, starting Friday this is what you're going to do from now on because I'm the boss. Now go." I wasn't building that kind of culture. I was building the exact opposite of that culture, actually, one that had essentially made me a lobbyist in my own company. I had to convince my people, from guards to top-level managers and HR personnel, that an idea was good for everyone before it could be implemented.

I thought it was somewhat hilarious. I used to come home and tell my wife, "Damn, I feel like I'm lobbying in Ottawa or Washington. I have to go to the staff, explain the pros and cons to them, tell them we piloted it, put them in touch with someone else who's already done it to show them the benefits, and then I might be able to convince them to make a change."

My wife would say, not surprisingly perhaps, "Why don't you just make the decision?"

But I couldn't do that. I had worked hard to turn my people into stakeholders by getting them involved in the decision-making process. This was the culture we had built, and I couldn't abide by it only when it was convenient and beneficial to me without undermining the whole effort.

So, while sometimes implementing large changes would take me a little longer, they were well vetted and challenged and better than my original idea; they were executed with all hands on deck. The new approach did wonders for my ability to see where my A-players were. I would watch them talk about the benefits, risks, and costs, all of which allowed me to see what kind of leader a person was, whether they liked change, and how well they could negotiate with others. All of these things were core to our business, and seeing them play out in full view allowed me to see pretty quickly whether a person was going to make it through or not. If they really dug their heels in, I'd ask myself why they were digging their heels in? I learned much more about everyone working for my company than I ever could have learned in the old "I'm the boss, do what I say" kind of model.

Our collaborative approach bonded us all in a more personal way. The president and CSO (chief support officer) and all leaders within the company had to spend more time together coaching people to get them through our process. You simply cannot build these types of relationships and solve problems as effectively when you hear from people reactively. If a manager only engages with their frontline people to write them up, then they have no real idea what their people need or want. If two heads are better than one, then how great can ten, twenty, a hundred be when you are all in alignment with a common goal and set of ideals? In my old management style at Source, I would tell people to bring me solutions, not problems. With the new style and models, if someone had a problem, I would first ask them if they had run through the collaboration process with everyone involved in the issue. If they had not, then they had to collaborate with those involved and come back to me with a solution everyone could agree on. We had worked hard to build a step-by-step collaboration process, and I made sure that everyone used it.

As a leader, you can't be the only one thinking about strategy without burning yourself out in a hurry. By creating a system that

> AS A LEADER, YOU CAN'T BE THE ONLY ONE THINKING ABOUT STRATEGY WITHOUT BURNING YOURSELF OUT IN A HURRY.

encouraged and supported people to collaborate and problem-solve, I no longer had to be the one figuring out every problem. Our people didn't just have their brains back; they had every brain in the company at their disposal to help find solutions or improvements within any corner of our operations. It afforded everyone a faster, more creative problem-solving process and a better work-life balance and subsequently gave us a competitive edge in our industry. In fact, we were able to pull so far ahead of everyone else in our market that no one could catch up to us. Companies in our industry had long been plagued by loyalty issues, but for us, our people would fight to stay. They wouldn't leave for a competitor because they could never get the type of responsibility and autonomy we gave them anywhere else. We gave everyone a voice at the table, and that's what any great employee really wants, no matter what their position. People at this point were solving problems better collectively and bringing issues to my attention that I didn't even know existed.

INSPECT WHAT YOU EXPECT

We had a new site coordinator managing the contract at the Nova Scotia Community College in Dartmouth, a bright young man named Liam Dawson. Once he was finally settled into the role, I decided to check in to see how he was faring.

I started off with the usual "Tell me a little bit about yourself. Where are you from, and what are your interests? What drew you to Source Security?" Then I got to my more pointed questions about his onboarding process. I was curious about his onboarding experience with other companies in our industry in regards to onboarding. Were we really blowing out the competition in this sector, as onboarding was a major industry pain point?

Liam immediately put a huge smile on my face. He responded that in all of his time in the security industry, working for several companies, he had never seen onboarding like ours before. He told me he clearly understood our purpose and values and what we were trying to achieve. I then asked if he had ever experienced this type of process in any other industry he had worked in, and he told me the only one that came to mind was FedEx. This is the type of feedback I had been longing to hear from my employees. If Source could be likened to the cultural caliber of FedEx, I knew we were onto something.

I asked Liam who he thought he reported to. This question caught him off guard. He really needed to think about his answer, and finally came out with "Well…the client?'

"Yes," I answered, "but who at Source Security do you report to?" I was curious if our upside-down org chart was clear to the front-line staff.

He paused for quite some time, and finally answered, "The staff, I suppose. I'm here to support them, and if they don't like my leadership, I know that based on this company's model, my job is in their hands."

I was thrilled with this response. All that came out of my mouth was "Yes, that's exactly right."

CHAPTER 10

TIME TO ASK MYSELF THE TOUGHEST QUESTION OF ALL

Ten years into running Source, I started to think about how we could save on costs, like most business owners. One idea was to reduce the cost of uniforms by cutting out the middleman and going directly to the manufacturer. All uniforms in Canada at least start in China, so I thought, "I'm going to go directly to China, get my own uniforms at a fraction of the cost, and go on a big adventure while I'm at it."

I caught a flight to Hong Kong with a translator. Before we left, we had been going back and forth with a few factories that were developing samples of an event uniform. For our old uniforms, I had ripped off the jersey design of a New Zealand rugby team—the Hurricanes, I think—and now I wanted to get my own design, one that no other company could replicate. In Canada, the cost just to create my own design would have been $85, while in China I was looking at about $6.95. With a fashionable and original design and quality production, our uniforms would go from being a major cost to actually being a profit center, because I could sell them to staff for $20 and make $10. Naturally, I was really keen on the idea of turning a profit out of a loss.

After we landed in China, we took a train to Shenzhen, where we planned to meet a man named Mr. Lao. Upon our arrival, Mr. Lao picked us up to begin our drive to a nearby factory. I got in the front seat, and my translator, a nice young lady named Anita, hopped in the back. Immediately, Mr. Lao began talking in Chinese, which Anita translated to me. "Mr. Lao says it is very nice to meet you. He says you're a very handsome young man."

Not certain of the customs, I said, "You tell Mr. Lao that it is very nice to meet him, too, and he's also very handsome."

Anita relayed my words to Mr. Lao, but as she did, I noticed a change in his tone and demeanor toward me as he relayed his reply to Anita. "Mr. Lao knows that he's not attractive at all, and he knows that you're lying, and this is a very bad way to start business."

I was left stumbling for words for a few moments, having both insulted our kind driver and potentially soured my first business relationship in China, all within the first few hours of being in the country.

"Oh my god," I said. "I didn't mean to offend him. Please tell him I am sorry."

Mr. Lao did look a bit like a frog, but I was just trying to use my Canadian etiquette to win some favor with people, like I did back home. This time, however, it bit me in the ass. It was a bad start with Mr. Lao, but we managed to turn it around and work out a great deal on our uniforms.

It was a valuable lesson for me, though, one that taught me the real value and importance of being honest even when you think it doesn't matter. An honest leader is one that people will follow with far less hesitation than one blowing smoke up their ass and speaking in code. As I learned from Mr. Lao, when you step outside of being completely honest with someone, it doesn't matter where you are or what's happening, you will get caught.

I took that lesson with me throughout my years with Source, and at a certain point, I had to be completely honest with myself.

After a decade and a half, my business had turned a huge corner. At thirty-seven, I had a great company and my work-life balance was amazing. I was doing more thinking and reading and attending more seminars than I ever could have done if I'd stayed in the weeds. I was spending less than 10 percent of my time actually in my business managing day-to-day tasks. Everything else was spent on business development, shaking things up, and coaching people. This is exactly what I had been longing to do in business. It was my dream job.

Yet I still yearned for a challenge. All the extra time allowed a lot of thought about the future to circulate through my head. My wife was pregnant at the time, so I knew if I was going to make a move, I had to do it quickly.

So, as I like to do, I went for a bike ride to get some alone time and think. Whenever I'm on a walk or ride, meditating, listening to music, or whatever else I can do to focus on as little as possible, that's when I ask myself really tough questions. The reason for that is because I'm not very good at seeing a solution if the answer is not black and white. If the answer to the question doesn't end in yes or no, or pass or fail, it is no good for my brain. For me it is all about getting to the right question. I truly believe that's one of our problems as leaders. It's not necessarily to problem-solve all the time, but to ask our stakeholders the right question and have them find the solution.

It's similar to if you were dating someone and asked yourself whether or not you really wanted to be with them anymore. If you approached that question with waffling logic like, "Well, I kind of like them, but if this could change and that could change, then maybe I'd like them more. Last week they *were* a little mean, though." No. That's a waste of time. Knowing what you know about your partner now, would you be excited to start dating them tomorrow, yes or no?

That's the type of question I need to make myself answer, as it allows me to make the most critical decisions.

I had climbed the ladder, we were successfully rattling our industry by building a national company of stakeholders, and now it was time to either jump to new heights or stay put. That is always a good place to be, but I'd be lying if I said it wasn't a little terrifying, too.

In my mind, there are really only three steps to that ladder, which are reached by asking a series of questions. The first set of questions are: "Knowing what I know about my company, if I were to buy my company with $1 million of my hard-earned retirement money, what would I do differently? What would I change about my business? Who would I keep as employees? What customers would I keep? What systems and processes would I keep? Would I keep my offices?" Those are all good questions that I had to evaluate first.

The second step I took was asking myself, "If I had to re-create my industry today, and I had a blank canvas and a brush, how would it look? How would it feel? How would I re-create this entire industry, knowing what I know about its challenges and pain points?"

I had asked myself these questions before, but I still hadn't made it to the third and final question, which was really the toughest of all for me. As I peddled faster and faster, it came to me: "Knowing what I know about my industry, would I be excited to reinvest in it today? If I were an investor, and some young buck entrepreneur approached me and said, 'Mr. Lovett, I have this great security company, and I would like you to invest in it,' what would I say?"

In an instant, almost like a reflex, I had my answer: "Absolutely NOT."

The revelation smacked me in the face. I almost ran off the bike path and into a tree. I knew I needed to move, and I needed to move. So, I decided to go to market.

Everything in business negotiations is about leverage. If you do not start with leverage, you're in trouble. You need to take a hard look not only at your actual leverage, but also at your perceived leverage. If you're a good negotiator, you start with as much leverage as you can, because it only dwindles from there. So, I thought of who the strategic buyers would be, and five came to mind. Within two weeks, I sent a package to all five buyers I thought would be interested, in the hopes of creating a bidding war.

Against the advice of most, I didn't want to use a broker. This was the biggest sale of my life, and I wasn't going to leave it to a brokerage or accounting firm. They could deal with the details, but I was going to fight the fight.

I started by sending a teaser. I sent our financial statements and some high-level information about our core customer group, what verticals we were in, and about ten other "need to know" snapshots about the company. Then, I sent a recast of our financials, which essentially told potential buyers what annual revenues would have looked like over the years with our current model and efficiencies in place. That changed our financials footprint in such a way that investors could better predict our future financial trajectory.

Within days, I had letters of intent from three potential buyers. This was all uncharted territory for me, however, so I was still anxious, even with three interested parties already at the table. When I got the first offer, I was shocked. I was out paddleboarding at the time, trying to burn off some of my anxiety. I had to get off my paddleboard once I got the offer because my knees went weak. I looked at the offer and whispered to myself, "Wow. That's a big number. That could change our life."

Three or four days later, another offer came in, and it was even higher. When the last offer came in, three or four days after that, it was the highest of them all. I was over the moon with excitement, but I was nervous, too. What would they do to my company? What would I do without Source? I had given myself more questions than I had answers.

People said, "Ron, that's how they start, but you'll never get those numbers. They'll come in and chop you down, and you'll never get a deal done." And again, I didn't listen. When I'd sent my letters to these companies, I wanted them to know I wasn't a reverse tire kicker. I wasn't playing around, so I told them very directly: "I'm having a child. I'm moving to Copenhagen in a few months. This deal has to be done before I move."

I offered to meet with the two parties that had given the top offers, but only if they came to Halifax. I wanted to know how committed they were, but even more, I wanted to show them what we had actually done. I needed to ensure they saw our model, our systems and processes, our culture and stakeholders. Otherwise, they would just be buying on numbers, and that wasn't going to present the complete value of our company. They needed to hear my story and see under the hood of this beautiful car we had built. If they did I knew they would be more motivated to complete the sale.

Fortunately, both companies came and listened to my presentation, which covered everything. By the end, both companies were impressed by how far ahead of the curve we were, and the company with the highest offer wanted me to sign a letter of intent. Such a letter would have barred me from negotiating with anyone else, so I decided to consult with one of my mentors, John Risley, who had lots of experience doing deals. On his advice, I went back to the table with the company offering the highest bid.

Negotiation is always about playing the right cards at the right time. You need to have a throwaway card, and that's the one you usually put down first to see what kind of room you can create for your more crucial cards. Thanks to my coaching from John, who is arguably one of the best negotiators in the country, my throwaway card was requesting a nonrefundable deposit. I said, "I'll sign your letter of intent, but if you're going to come in and do due diligence with my company, look at all my financial statements, etc., then you'll know everything about me. I want a nonrefundable deposit of $250,000." That wasn't really done in my industry, at least not in private deals, and I knew that.

To no surprise, they rejected my request. So, I showed them the card I really wanted. I said, "No problem. If you're not going to do that, then I need you to take out the exclusivity clause." Taking out exclusivity meant that I could continue to negotiate with other parties during the due diligence process, a condition to which this company agreed. That gave me the leverage I needed to get the other parties to raise their offers.

I whittled the parties down to one based on two things: who overpromised and under delivered on timelines, and who seemed to appreciate our company's model the least. It was important that I showed as much value as possible, and that value was in our culture, our people, our systems, and our processes. I had already investigated and studied the systems of the buyers, so I would show them our model and theirs side by side. "What do you do for client-specific onboarding?" I might ask. And I'd hear the same story. Then I would show them their system next to ours, highlighting the costs, hours, training requirements, necessary management structure, and more. In all cases, our systems were several times more efficient than theirs. By having our systems in place, they would save money and time, which gave me substantial negotiating leverage.

The party that remained at the table happened to be the largest security company in North America and from the United States. I held a dinner at a restaurant in Halifax with their vice president from Canada, their company president from America, their vice president of mergers and acquisitions, and three accountants from a third-party accounting firm in New York. On the other side of the table, it was just me. No one at the other company knew me, which is to say that none of them knew how outrageous I am. As we began to talk, I could tell that everyone was a little stiff. I like being a little outrageous to break the ice, but I decided to wait for the perfect opportunity.

I asked them, "What makes you different in the industry?"

They looked around at each other and one of their team replied, "Well, we're really good at working with anyone's budgets. If someone has a budget for security and all they have is a certain number, we'll find a solution to fit that budget. So, we're very creative like that."

I thought, *Okay, this is my time. Here I come.* "That's great," I said. "We try to be really creative with budgets, too. In fact, we always try to come at things from a totally different angle. So for clients that don't have a full budget for security, we executed a little person security team that would be half the price of a regular security team." I stopped right there, maintaining a deadpan face. Everyone looked stunned and confused. I waited, letting the awkward moment of silence grow more and more uncomfortable. People's jaws slowly dropped, and the whole table stopped eating their food. Then I suddenly burst out laughing, and the entire team, no doubt relieved, exploded with laughter.

I love to torture people like that to see what they're made of and how well our minds will work together. Though it is a little risky, it is my personality. Plus, it got them to understand, in a matter of minutes, who they were dealing with. It was also important to me that we established some kind of human relationship rather than communicating explicitly through lawyers. I prefer old school, face-to-face handshakes and eye contact type relationships, so after dinner I said to their VP of mergers and acquisitions, "Let's commit to one thing that is crucially important, and that is, I really want to make sure we communicate in a timely fashion. Let's commit to how soon we'll get back to each other. Because if this deal goes and the lawyers are back and forth on an item, it is costing us both money. If that happens, let's also commit to getting on the phone and sorting it out as human beings so we can move to the next level." Their VP agreed, and I held her accountable to that commitment of communication. That was critical in this deal.

The other thing I did was work to provide myself with a bigger stack of cards while we were negotiating. Every deal has to be win/win, so the more things you can offer a buyer or seller that does not cost you much, the better the deal will be for you. I wanted to know my options, as well as theirs, because I was aware that everyone has their actual leverage and their perceived leverage. What is valuable to me may not necessarily be valuable to them, so I had to really be sensitive and aware of what their other options were.

Soon the negotiations turned into a game of chicken. Sometimes I'd say, "You know what? That's not going to work for me. This deal's done." Then I'd go upstairs and rock myself back and forth sucking my thumb, hoping they'd come back to the table. They were a big organization, so they moved much slower. That delay frightened the hell out of me several times and made managing my emotions difficult, as I had to be both patient and aggressive at the same time. But sure enough, they always came back and we would move past it.

I would also try to be as objective as I could in the negotiations, using words like "This is what I feel is reasonable for both parties." For every suggestion I put in, I tried to see from their response what was important to them. That helped give me a better position. When you know what a party wants and needs, you have so much more leverage to work with because you can create or highlight the ways in which you can deliver those things.

Perhaps it is my nature. Maybe it is my upbringing. Most likely, it is a combination of both, but for whatever reason, I'm aggressive in my business dealings. So when the lawyers were stuck at a point and I couldn't get in touch with my contact at the firm, I would call their lawyer in California myself. The first time I did, their lawyer was caught off guard. "Oh, hey, Mr. Lovett," he said. "Uh, well, this is very strange. I have never talked to the seller on the other side. We're not really supposed to be talking."

I didn't hesitate. "Yeah, I know, but, look, let's just chat about this for a second. We'll get it figured out, and then we can keep moving forward."

That happened two or three times, and while it freaked out their lawyer, my lawyer had a chuckle because he knew how aggressive I am. I was stick handling the deal every step of the way, and by doing so, I learned more than I ever could have from any business school.

We closed the deal the first week of November, just three months after I announced the sale. But what I was most happy about with regard to the deal was the value I was able to get for Source. Our industry was generally trading at a two to five times multiple. Garda Security, one of the largest security companies in North America with nearly $1 billion in revenue, took their company from publicly traded to private at a seven times multiple. I had met with Marc-André Aubé, Garda's COO at the time, just before taking Source to market. "Ron, if you ever want to sell, I can write you a check for five times all day long. I could do it right here at lunchtime," he said. "Six would be tough, because we went public to private at seven times. I could never get you seven. Forget it. You're a multimillion dollar company, which is nothing compared to a billion-dollar company."

I always kind of remembered that, and I knew that everyone— my lawyer, my accountant, my colleagues, everyone—thought I was crazy for thinking I could achieve more than those numbers. But I did. In fact, I ended up getting a twenty-four times multiple of EBITA in an industry that was trading at a multiple of three to five times. To me, following the standards simply because they were the standards was what was really crazy. That price really spoke to the alignment we had as a team; the systems, the processes, and the focus that we had; and our core customer. We didn't build a company with a nest egg of inherited capital. We built a high-value company from scratch simply by thinking outside the box and introducing a unique model that solved internal and external industry problems. All of those things lined up in the end, and the value we achieved in dollar amounts was essentially validation for our efforts. All of our work and creativity had a price tag, and it was a big one. I was really happy about that.

This wasn't some technology company. This was a brick-and-mortar security company that had great systems and a culture that was unheard of in our industry (or across many other industries, for that matter), and one of the largest companies in our industry paid us for it. I was thirty-seven years old and I felt like I had won the Olympics in every event. For me, it was a validation of all the work I had dedicated nearly half my life to. Not to mention that throughout all of those years, I was just trying to do what other people were not doing. Now they wanted to do what I was doing.

But believe it or not, what made me happiest of all was how our team members shone throughout the entire process. We had fifteen hundred stakeholders across the country at the time of these negotiations, and part of my due diligence was to take the buyers to a site and have them talk to my people. "You ask them what makes us better than everybody else," I said. So an entire team of executives went out to meet some of our security guards, and they could not believe that the frontline team members were saying the exact same thing as I had relayed the previous day. They thought maybe I had coached them on what to say. I was so proud to listen in, because what I heard time and again was our people telling stories about what they had created or accomplished as a result of our model. That was my BHAG, and I had never felt more at peace, more complete and proud, in my professional career as I did listening to those conversations between my team and these executives.

In Source's first ten years, people would have been buying Ron Lovett, his Rolodex, and the few things that he could do. But through selling Source, I got a chance to see what had been achieved over the last five years of our transformation. The buyer wasn't buying me anymore. They were buying a company filled with top talent. They were buying a well-oiled machine the CEO really didn't have to tend to on a day-to-day basis. The CEO of Source was more or less a cheerleader in the background, suggesting things the company could do. With most companies, the owner is key to the operations; they would have to come with the business in a sale. But I wasn't the company anymore, and I had succeeded in setting up a business that way was incredibly rewarding—not to mention liberating. My ego was no longer there to say, "This is *my* business." I was very proud of saying, "This is *our* business and I really have nothing to do with it anymore." That's a really nice thing for a founder to say, that his or her company has taken a life of its own and doesn't need them anymore. Source didn't need my organs anymore. It had its own body and its own life, and it was organically doing its own thing.

Of course, there was more to my decision to sell Source. The industry itself is stressful, as is any commoditized industry. As much as some potential clients always said, "We want to know what's different with you," most didn't care about anything but price. That could be frustrating. Even though we created something really impactful, I still wasn't passionate about the security industry itself.

Today I'm really excited about the future, because I feel like the handcuffs are completely off. To do what Source was able to do in an industry that I didn't even really enjoy, I was interested to find out what I could do with something that I do love.

That meant looking in the mirror and asking myself what I am passionate about. "What do I love? What gets me up in the morning?" I asked myself. I came up with three things, none of which was in my current industry. One is my love of connecting people. I was doing that outside of my business, but not in my business. The other thing I love is problem solving. I'm passionate about it. I love trying to figure out people's problems. And at this point, I feel I have a knack for it. Our customers in security didn't really want us to solve their problems; they wanted us to monitor their problems. They wanted us to log in and do things the way they wanted them done. We built so many core, simple, scalable, and sustainable processes and systems that we could plug into any company to solve a lot of their problems, and I felt frustrated that we were unable to do that in our industry. And finally, I love learning. I had hit the ceiling with my company, and I knew I could no longer grow if I stayed. I was growing externally, so I knew it was time to follow my interests in a way that would allow me to be more dedicated to them. All three of these passions add up to what I perceive as my best skill: alignment. My ability to connect with people and to solve problems, and my curiosity for learning new things gave me the tools I needed to align a company's culture, purpose, and service, which was perhaps my greatest achievement at Source.

So the next chapter for me is building a new company brick by brick. I realized that it wasn't the fact that we were security experts that made Source so successful—because we weren't. We were so successful because we were able to turn disgruntled frontline employees into passionate stakeholders. I decided to launch a consulting firm around these same systems, processes, and culture to align companies properly. This time around, I won't take ten years trying to figure out who my true core customer is and why, or to build an incredible culture. We're only willing to work with companies that are looking to truly become aligned, by giving their employees their brains back, and uncovering untapped potential. Providing value to other businesses and their leaders by coaching them on the lessons I learned and the model I used to build Source meets all of my passions in one package, and that is extremely rare. I know that if we were able to accomplish greatness in the security industry, we can help any business do the same.

But this time around, things have become a little more personal for me. I named my consulting firm Connolly Owens, weaving past values with present from the two men I admire most. My grandfather, James Connolly, who was a Speaker of the House, carried himself with grace in the business community. James Connolly was known for always helping those in need, and blurring the lines between business and community. And my wife's father, Bob Owens, who is undoubtedly the king of kings when it comes to building a successful value-based company, while always putting his family first. Bob seems to do the *right* thing every time, and I didn't know that was possible. His North Star follows him from his work to his home each day, and then wakes up with him the next. You see, the learning never stops. Each time, we get better from the last, and we find people not to emulate but to learn from.

I think life is about change. Change is what keeps us excited to be alive, as it has the potential to provide us with the most rewarding growth. I was always very envious of entrepreneurs who talked about selling this company and that company, because it takes a lot of guts. After selling Source, I'm confident that it takes ten times more guts to sell your business than it does to start it. I really wanted the experience of selling a company, because I wanted to know how it was done. I also wanted to know that I could handle it. I love solving problems, but I love helping others solve their problems even more. There is so much more satisfaction from it, and now I know I'm capable of coaching others through the process. That in itself makes the experience worth it to me.

> IT TAKES TEN TIMES MORE GUTS TO SELL YOUR BUSINESS THAN IT DOES TO START IT.

Alas, there is no way to avoid the pain of leaving a company you spent your adult life building. I had done a three-month transitional agreement with the purchaser to help integrate the companies properly. On my last day, I scheduled a conference call and invited everyone in the company to join. For years, I typically did monthly, company-wide updates by phone in which I explained what was new with the company, the wins we had, the challenges we had, and so on. So, I decided it was only fitting to do a final call on my final day and tell everyone goodbye. I scheduled the call for 2 p.m., and over lunch I decided to give a summary of Source's history and recount some of my favorite stories from over the years. I wanted everyone to know what they had been involved in accomplishing.

I went over the highs and lows of Source's history, from the night Jack Tobin was stabbed to the horrific night when guards Jontia Whynder and Romain Provo died in a car accident, to our most entertaining moments and industry-changing successes.

As I was talking, I started choking up. By the middle of the call, I was bawling like a child and regretting that I had made this a company-wide conference call. But then I began to talk about the moment I really turned into a true leader, which was when I was able to be vulnerable. This call, I realized, was the final vulnerable moment for me, and the most vulnerable of all. I could not keep myself together during the call, and as my emotions took over, I had to excuse myself multiple times. But I was able to come back each time and finally finish my speech. "I can't believe what we have done," I told them at the end. "I will miss you all. Thank you."

My inbox was flooded immediately after I finished with well-wishes and heartfelt notes, making the experience one of the most memorable moments of my life. I had worked to build a culture in which I could be vulnerable with my people, so seeing their president and chief support officer enveloped in such a sincere moment, comfortable being so emotional with them, was a befitting end, I think. It felt like we were an NFL team that had won the Super Bowl, and my time was done. We had celebrated so many victories together through the years, but we had finally won the big game, and everyone was very happy that we did it together. I might have led them there, but they were happy for me and proud of themselves for reaching our ultimate goal. Seeing me go on to my next chapter in life was a celebration of a major victory rather than mourning a loss. And that's exactly the way I wanted it to end. After that fifteen-year rollercoaster ride, I had nothing left but tears for my team, my family. We spent the day just as I had hoped, recapping the story of how we changed an industry against all odds—and we were reminded that we did it by helping each other change ourselves.

NEW LIFE, NEW JOB

It was perfect timing, really. As the sale of Source was nearing finality, my wife, Natalie, gave birth to a baby girl. Of course, it wouldn't be an experience free of trouble—as long as I had anything to do with it, anyway.

As Natalie lay in the hospital in pain, she desperately passed the responsibility of filling out the birth certificate to me, her dyslexic and ADHD-ridden husband. A nurse led me to a computer in the hallway and instructed me to enter our baby's legal name into the blanks on the screen. Natalie knows I cannot spell worth a damn, so she exhaustedly asked me to spell the name before I went out to the computer. Hardheaded as I am, I just laughed and said, "Honey, you have nothing to worry about. I got this." I stood at the computer and began entering my daughter's first name. *Georgia,* I wrote. For her middle name I wrote *James,* after my grandfather. And for her last name, I wrote *Lovett.* No problem, I thought. Easy. But then I saw a section marked "Other." Of course, I assumed this special tempting box was presenting itself to me so that I could document her nickname we had come up with during the days leading up to her birth. I had been calling her "Little G" for the last forty-eight hours, so I thought, "Oh, well, I'll write 'Little G' into the nickname section for fun."

We took our daughter home the following day, and I didn't think any more about the name registration until a few weeks later when my wife approached me with our daughter's newly arrived health card in hand.

"Ron," she said sharply.

"Yes, honey," I said, trying to sweeten the tone.

"Why in the hell is our daughter named 'Georgia J. L. Lovett'?"

I had to think for a minute, because I had no idea how that could be the case—until it finally hit me. "Oh my God," I thought to myself, "they actually used the *Little G*." I obviously denied it right away to my wife. I thought maybe I could get it changed without her being the wiser, but a few hours later, Natalie came back and said she had a feeling I wasn't telling her something. So I confessed and explained that when I filled out her birth certificate, I listed her first name as Georgia, middle name James, last name Lovett, and in the section marked "Other" I typed in "Little G."

Natalie narrowed her eyes at me and said, "Are you telling me our daughter's legal name is Georgia James Little G f***ing Lovett?"

I smiled shyly and said, "Unfortunately, yes, honey. Yes, it is."

"Ron!"

Poor name choices aside, being a dad has been the greatest achievement of my life. Little G has already taught me more than I can probably ever teach her, but I will never stop trying. So, to you I say this: Don't just build a great company. Build a great life. Build it with meaning and purpose. Be daring but humble, and live in gratitude of the achievements that others have helped you create and the joys they have allowed you to experience. Because when you do, success will be a constant no matter what you do, no matter where you decide to go from here.

ABOUT THE AUTHOR

Ron Lovett was the president and founder of Source Security & Investigations, which was a leading national physical security services company based in Halifax, Nova Scotia Canada. An entrepreneur and leader with a passion for change, Ron is passionate in his mission to develop culture that aligns people to one common purpose. He is a father, husband, speaker, and constant learner who lives life to the fullest. Ron is now the founder and chairman of Connolly Owens, a company that provides an alignment program which converts employees into passionate stakeholders for large corporations. For more inquiries please visit www.connollyowens.com.

To inquire about speaking engagements or bulk orders of this book, contact Ron Lovett at ronlovett@connollyowens.com.

Made in the USA
Columbia, SC
18 January 2019